Great PILLOWS!

Fabric Painting
Simple Sewing
Cross-Stitch
Embroidery
Applique
Quilting
Crochet

Great
PILLOWS!

60
Original
Projects

Chris Rankin

Illustrations by Diane Weaver

Sterling Publishing Co., Inc.   New York
A Sterling/Lark Book

Editor: Dawn Cusick
Art Director: Chris Bryant
Production: Elaine Thompson, Chris Bryant
Proofreading: Julie Brown
Translations: Irene M. Selent Language Services
Library of Congress Cataloging-in-Publication Data
Available

10 9 8 7 6 5 4 3 2 1

A Sterling/Lark Book

First paperback edition published in 1996 by
   Sterling Publishing Company, Inc.
   387 Park Avenue South, New York, N.Y. 10016

Created and produced by Altamont Press, Inc.
   50 College Street, Asheville, NC 28801

© 1995 by Altamont Press

Distributed in Canada by Sterling Publishing
   c/o Canadian Manda Group, One Atlantic Avenue, Suite 105
   Toronto, Ontario, Canada M6K 3E7
Distributed in Great Britain and Europe by Cassell PLC
   Wellington House, 125 Strand, London WC2R 0BB, England
Distributed in Australia by Capricorn Link (Australia) Pty Ltd.
   P.O. Box 6651, Baulkham Hills, Business Centre, NSW 2153, Australia

Every effort has been made to ensure that all the information in this book is accurate.
However, due to differing conditions, tools, and individual skills, the publisher cannot be
responsible for any injuries, losses, and other damages which may result from the use of the
information in this book.

Sterling ISBN 0-8069-3162-0 Trade
            0-8069-3163-9 Paper

contents

INTRODUCTION

Pillows are a rare and wondrous decorating item ~ they fit in well with any personality, in any home. If you keep a pristine home, pillows are the perfect way to tie all the design schemes together, and giving the pillows a good straightening and fluffing every time you pass by will make you feel much better. If, on the other hand, you're a casual sort of person with a casual home to match, pillows are also just right for you ~ just spread them about any which way. Even children have a natural love of pillows. When they aren't enjoying them in the traditional manner, they're stacking them up to make forts or enjoying the proverbial pillow fight.

For needlework lovers, pillows make an ideal way to show-case finished pieces. Or, if you've always admired a craft such as cutwork, but don't have the time to make that exquisite bedspread or tablecloth you saw in a magazine, then just down scale the project to a pillow front for a manageable time investment that you'll enjoy for years. Pillows also make wonderful, custom gifts. When you're in a sewing mood, it's easy to whip out several extras.

Probably what pillows do best, though, is invite. They are the welcome mat of interior design, adding warmth and comfort by their very presence. They are the ultimate symbol of luxury, and there aren't very many luxuries in life as inexpensive as a pillow. So, sit back with a mug of your favorite hot drink, flip through the pages that follow, and change your life with pillows.

Pillows are one of the few interior design renovations that can be completed quickly. A couch full of great pillows can be assembled in less time than it takes to repaint the trim work in your living room. Pillows are a wonderful way to experiment with different fabrics, prints, and styles, allowing you to live with a new look for a while before going to the time and expense of reupholstering a couch or making new curtains.

Making Pillows

Pillows are one of those wonderful sewing endeavors that can be as complicated or as simple as you like. From sewing to stuffing, a simple, two-piece pillow construction can take less than an hour to complete. The more details you choose to add, the more rewarding the process and the more enjoyable the finished project. For more elaborate pillows, peruse the appendix section for an inspirational review of basic needlework and quilting techniques.

Materials

Oh, for the good old days, when pillows were made from worn-out clothing and stuffed with the same. Nowadays, choosing materials is a little more time consuming. If you're experimenting with a new color or pattern scheme, opt for the most inexpensive materials you can find. For pillows you envision becoming a permanent part of your life, buy the best fabric you can afford. Economizing is still possible: purchase just enough of the premium fabric for the front panel and purchase a contrasting, less expensive fabric for the back side, or fill the pillow with an inexpensive stuffing and replace it as needed.

FABRICS

Fiber content, pattern, and weave are all important elements of fabric choice. For the most part, feel free to choose whatever you like, taking heed to the following potential dangers.

Beware of bright, cheerful colors that may well bleed their bright colors all over your expensive couch. Always wash fabrics first and then color-test by gently rubbing a small piece of white felt against the dry fabric.

If using contrasting fabrics for the pillow back or a ruffle, be sure to check the fiber contents first. Although many professional designers consider it a bad idea to mix fabrics with different fiber contents, you can get away with it as long as their laundering requirements are the same.

Fabrics with loose, grainy weaves should always be lined with a fabric of tighter weave to prevent stretching and unraveling.

FILLS

Technically, anything that transforms a flat fabric form into a three-dimensional piece can work as stuffing, but your concerns will probably include comfort, price, and durability.

Stitches

The variety of stitching options available to pillow makers shouldn't be intimidating, even for beginning sewers. Every one of these stitches — even a zigzag — can be used to make a pillow, but choosing the right stitch for the job ensures more professional results.

BASTING STITCHES

Basting stitches are loose, running stitches (usually done by hand) that are used instead of pins to hold fabrics together during machine stitching. It doesn't matter what color thread you use — in fact, sometimes a totally incompatible color makes the stitches easier to see come removal time. Use basting stitches for hard-to-sew corners, when working with slippery fabrics, or when you just want more control.

STAYSTITCHING

Staystitching is used to prevent the fabric from stretching during the pinning and sewing process. Staystitches are usually just a single row of running machine stitches along the seam allowance at your regular stitch length and tension. Staystitching is especially valuable for fabrics that will endure a lot of handling during a needlework process.

GATHERING STITCHES

Gathering stitches are used to evenly distribute excess fabric when one of the two fabrics in a seam is longer than the other. Sometimes, as with a sleeve cap, the difference is minimal, and gathers are used to add ease. Other times, such as when working with a ruffle, one length of fabric may be twice as long as the other.

Latex Foam is the best choice for pillows that will frequently withstand sitting weight. It's definitely worth the extra cost for a pillow that will be used a lot.

Polyester Foam is less expensive than Latex, but definitely worth the savings if the pillow will just sit pretty, or if you make the pillow with a zipper or overlapping back so the foam can be replaced when it starts to sag.

Stuffing allows you to be more spontaneous with shapes and sizes. A handful of stuffing can be worked into any shape detail in a pillow. You can purchase polyester or cotton stuffings, or recycle old clothing or stockings. If you choose to use recycled clothing, be sure to remove any snaps, buttons, or zippers first.

To make gathering stitches, first set the stitch length to its longest setting and stitch two rows about 1/4 inch from each other, the first one on the seam allowance measurement and the second one 1/4 inch outside the first, closest to the fabric's edge. To gather, gently pull the top or bottom threads, taking care to pull them evenly so both rows of stitches receive equal tension.

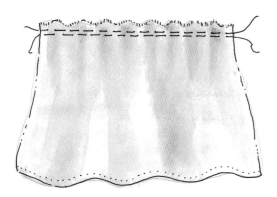

To gather long areas, divide both lengths of fabric into several smaller sections (such as into thirds or fourths) and mark them with pins, then just gather until the pins match.

TOPSTITCHING

Topstitching is usually done for decorative reasons in a matching or contrasting thread color. The stitch should be about 1/4 inch in from the edge and just a little longer than you use for regular seams to ensure ease. Extra rows of parallel topstitches can be added for a custom look. Be sure to press the garment or item before stitching.

ZIGZAG STITCHING

This versatile stitch can be decorative or functional. On a decorative level, zigzagging with a contrasting color of thread adds a fun flair to children's and contemporary projects. On the purely functional level, zigzagging the edges of loosely woven fabrics can prevent an epidemic of unravelling that can fatally injure pillow seams.

SLIPSTITCHING

This stitch (also known as Blindstitching) is used when you need to secure several layers together with the stitches invisible on both sides. In this book, most of the pillows call for slipstitching to close the small area of a seam left unsewn so the fabric can be turned right side out and stuffed.

Before you begin the stitches, gently press the fabric under so the seam allowances match. Then, begin by picking up several fabric threads just below the folded edge. Arrange the thread's knot so that it's inside the seam and doesn't show.

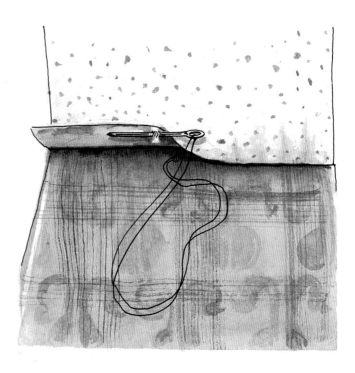

Slip the needle inside the fold about 1/4 inch directly above the stitches you just put on the needle, then bring the needle out and pick up a few more threads below the fold. Continue until you've secured all of the unsewn area.

Basic Assembly

Fortunately, there are enough ways to assemble pillows to suit every sewer's skill level and every designer's taste level. If you're just starting out, you will probably want to make several very basic pillows first, and then move on to the adaptations and embellishments that encompass other methods.

If sewing skill level is not a consideration, then you'll probably wish to choose a construction method that will suit your future pillow's lifestyle. For pillows made from inexpensive fabrics that won't be heavily used, the Simplest Pillow assembly (or a variation) is probably the best use of your time. If the pillow will require occasional or frequent laundering, then you should probably choose the Overlapped Back Pillow.

THE SIMPLEST PILLOW

This basic construction can be completed in under 30 minutes. First, pin two precut fabric shapes together with their right sides facing. Stitch all four sides (assuming you're working with a square or rectangle), leaving an opening large enough for turning. The opening's width should be determined by how you plan to fill out the pillow. If you're using a stuffing material, the opening can be as small as 4 inches (10 cm). If you're using a purchased pillow form, you'll need to play with the form in advance to see how small an opening you can get away with. Most pillow forms can be bent in half before inserting, so your opening can be slightly larger than half the form's width. When in doubt, it's better to leave too large rather than too small an opening. An opening that's too large will require just a few extra minutes of slipstitching. An opening that's too small may stretch or tear the fabric.

OPENING FOR TURNING

The next step is to turn the pillow right sides out. To do this, just pretend the pillow is an article of clothing that's inside out. Stick your hand or a few fingers through the opening, grab onto the fabric on the opposite edge, and pull the pillow out over your hand. Gently push the corners outward with a sharp, but not too sharp, object. (The points on a pair of dull children's scissors will work fine, but the points on your best shears will probably put holes in the fabric.) If the corners resist coming out into fine points, turn the pillow back inside out and trim or clip the corners to about 1/8 inch (3 mm) from the seam.

After filling the pillow with stuffing or a form, the only remaining task is to close the opening as inconspicuously as possible. The best choice for this task is the slipstitch, which, when worked well, secures the seam together and disappears from sight. Before you begin slipstitching, it makes sense to push the stuffing or pillow form as far away from the open end as possible. Then fold the raw edges under the same amount as your seam allowance and pin in place.

THE OVERLAPPED BACK PILLOW

This form of pillow construction often scares beginners away. (Quite needlessly, it should be pointed out.) The pillow is assembled from a single front fabric piece and from two separate back pieces. The back pieces are cut to the same width as the pillow front, but their lengths are cut several inches too long to form an overlap in the finished pillow. This overlap provides you with a clever way to insert and remove the pillow form, and there's no leftover seam opening that needs slipstitching!

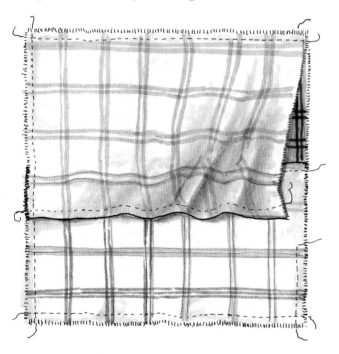

To assemble this type of pillow, place the pillow front on a flat surface with its right side facing up. Place one of the pillow back pieces on top of the front, with right sides facing, then place the second pillow back piece in place. The corners and corner edges should line up perfectly, but the two ends will overlap at some point. Hem the overlapping edges, then stitch all four seams. Turn the pillow right side out through the overlapped opening. Insert the pillow and adjust the opening so it lies flat.

Fun Variations

RUFFLES

Adding a ruffle is not a complicated process, but for good results it does require some attention to detail. Fabric strips for ruffles can be cut on the straight grain of the fabric or on the bias. Bias cuts, although they use up a lot more fabric, add a wonderful flair to fabrics with geometric prints.

To make a ruffle, hem one of the long edges of your ruffle strip. Add gathering stitches along the other long edge and gather until the ruffle strip fits the pillow, taking care to distribute the gathers as evenly as possible. Carefully pin the right side of the ruffle to the right side of the pillow front. (If your pillow doesn't have a definite front or back, then it won't matter which side you pin the ruffle to.) Allow for a little extra fullness at the corners and a seam allowance where the two short edges meet. Unpin just enough of the ruffle to allow you to stitch the short edges together, then repin.

RIGHT SIDE

If you're new to ruffles, you will probably want to stitch the ruffle to the pillow front at this point. The pillow back is then stitched to the front with right sides facing as though it were an ordinary pillow. Expèrienced pillow makers will often sew all three layers together in one step instead of two. If you choose this method, be sure to place the pins horizontally with their heads facing inside the pillow to ensure safe passage for your sewing machine's needle and make pin removal a simple task.

Although all of the ruffled pillows in this book call for a single hemmed layer of fabric, you always have the option of making a doubled ruffle. To do this, simply double the ruffle width and fold the fabric in half lengthwise with wrongs sides facing. Press flat. From this point on you just work with the doubled ruffle exactly as you would a single ruffle. Doubled ruffles will disappoint you in only two circumstances: if you try to use a very heavy fabric or if you skip the pressing step.

TUFTING

Tufted pillows look especially lovely when displayed with a variety of other assembly techniques. The tufting can be done by pulling the pillow layers together with several loops of thread or by sewing a button through all the layers. You'll have the best luck if you add tufting to a pillow that's been stuffed with a cooperative fill material (as opposed to a firm pillow form), and if you use a long needle and upholstery or quilting thread.

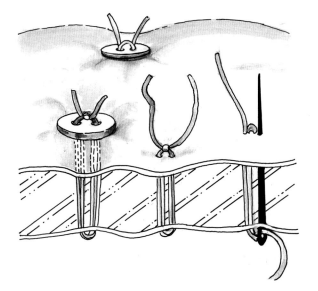

CORDING

Cording adds a polished, designer look to pillows, and gives one last chance to jazz them up with a bias stripe or a contrasting color. Like ruffles, the cording is simply sewn into the seam with the pillow front and back pieces. The only

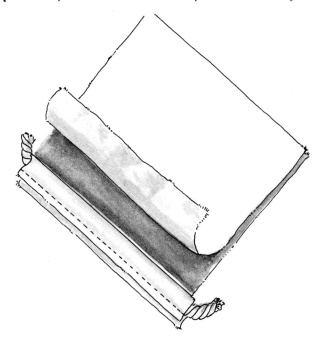

real trick is to take a lot of care during the pinning stage to make sure the cording will be taut in the seam. It's well worth your time to work slowly, and if you're adding a ruffle at the same time, 15 minutes of hand basting will prevent a lot of dissatisfaction.

Details, Details, Details...

When you're hot on the trail of finishing a pillow project, it can be tempting to sail through as quickly as possible. (After all, you might reason, unlike a piece of clothing, there's little chance someone will ever see your pillow seams.) A few extra minutes of care can make all the difference, though, and a few extra trim details, such as cording or a ruffle, can ward off the dreaded Pillow Boredom Syndrome for an extra few years.

BIAS STRIPS

Bias strips can be made at home to use in place of store-bought bias tape binding. The strips are cut on the bias because fabric cut on this angle has more natural "give" to it. To cut your own strips, place a single layer of pressed fabric on a flat surface and begin cutting from one corner across the diagonal to the other.

Continue cutting strips from the fabric to the left and to the right of your first cut. The strips should be about an inch wide, and can be stitched together to form the desired length.

Bias strips can also be used to create custom cording. Just place a length of plain cording in the center of a bias strip. Fold the right sides over to encase the cord and stitch close to the cord.

SEAM TRIMMING

Seams are usually trimmed to eliminate excess bulk, which makes turning easier. It's especially important to trim seams when using heavy fabrics. Be careful not to trim closer than 1/8 inch away from the seam to prevent unraveling.

CURVED SEAMS

Curves are a challenge for even experienced sewers, probably because it's just so much fun speeding along that anything forcing you to slow down poses a challenge. The key is to work slowly and to gently guide the fabric where you want it to go. Sometimes you may need to stop the machine, lift the presser foot with the needle through the fabric, and guide the fabric in the correct direction.

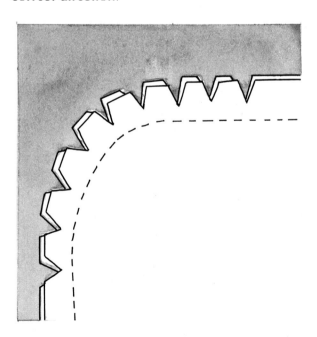

To make turning easier and to make the seam more pressable, make several clips into curved seams.

MITERING

Mitering is used at the corners of pillow borders as a finishing technique. Mitering can be awkward until you get the technique down, so you may wish to study the illustrations well and then practice with basting stitches before proceeding.

First, turn the seam allowance or the hem and facing to the inside and press. Open out the pressed edges. Fold the corner diagonally across the point so the pressed lines meet, then press.

Open the corner and trim it 1/4 inch from the crease. With right sides facing, fold the corner, matching the trimmed edges.

Stitch on the diagonal crease. Trim the fold at the point and press the seam open. Turn and press well. If you're in a hurry or don't have the temperament to learn how to miter, refer to the pillow instructions on page 86 for an alternative method.

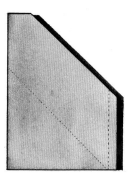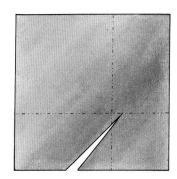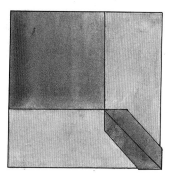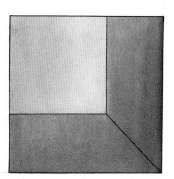

TRANSFERRING DESIGNS

Several of the pillow projects in this book instruct you to transfer a pattern or motif to a pillow front. The tried-and-true dressmaker's carbon method still works fine, but you may wish to explore the newer transfer methods available in most sewing departments.

When working with transfer pencils, trace the design onto heavy tracing paper. Turn the paper over and trace over your marks with the transfer pencil. Position the paper, traced side down, on the right side of your fabric. Gently secure the corners of the tracing paper to the fabric with sewing pins. Preheat your iron to a low setting and press the iron over all of the traced areas for a few seconds. Be careful to use only straight up and down motions; sliding the iron back and forth will smudge your image.

When working with transfer paper, place the paper over the fabric and then position your motif on top of the paper. Trace over the pattern outlines and remove the paper. A hard surface and a sharp-pointed pen will increase the quality of your results. Follow the manufacturer's instructions for removing the tracings, and always pretest your fabric to ensure success.

Ruffled Delights

Nothing says easy living like an assortment of ruffled pillows in cool summer fabrics. For a softer look, consider making the ruffles with a decorative eyelet edging.

MATERIALS
FOR EACH PILLOW

- 1-1/2 yards (1.4 m) cotton fabric
- stuffing

INSTRUCTIONS

For the heart-shaped pillow, enlarge the pattern 165% and cut it out. For the second pillow, cut out two 16-inch (41 cm) squares. For either pillow, cut out a 128-inch (269 cm) length of 3-1/2-inch-wide (8 cm) fabric for the ruffle, piecing if necessary.

Stitch two rows of basting stitches on one long edge of the ruffle strip. Hem the remaining long edge. Gather the ruffle to fit the pillow, then pin or hand-baste it to the right side of the pillow back. With right sides facing, stitch all four edges together, leaving a small opening for stuffing. Turn right sides out and stuff the pillow, then slipstitch the opening closed.

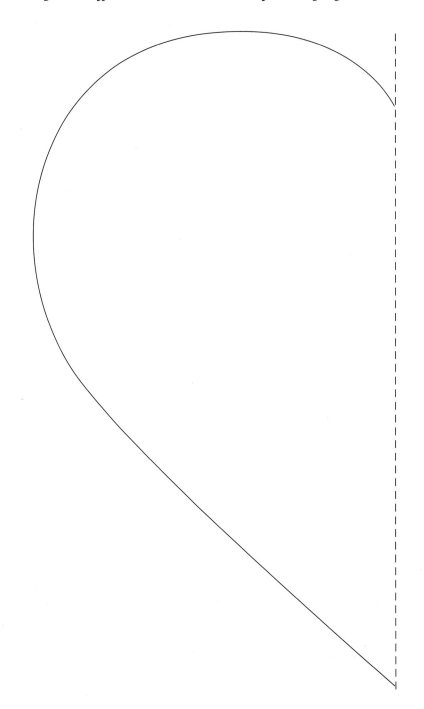

Hexagon Patchwork

Instead of the traditional hexagon piecing techniques, this pillow uses a deceptively simple method to achieve perfect corners.

MATERIALS

- scraps of cotton prints
- sheet of thin cardboard
- craft knife
- paper clips
- 1/8 yard (.1 m) backing fabric
- stuffing
- 16-inch (41 cm) length of 5/8-inch-wide (15 mm) grosgrain ribbon

INSTRUCTIONS

Trace and cut out 19 whole hexagon and 12 half-hexagon patterns from the cardboard. Cut out 19 whole hexagons and 12 half-hexagons from the fabric prints. Working on a padded surface, cut away the indicated areas with a craft knife to create support frames.

Place the cardboard frames on the wrong side of the fabric shapes. Fold the hems at the top and bottom over the cardboard and secure with a paper clip. Then fold the remaining hems over, one at a time, and secure the corners with a couple of stitches.

Working on the wrong side of the shapes, whipstitch the hexagons to each other. In the areas where three hexagons meet, take up the outer point of each and work a buttonhole stitch to create one smooth area. Press well, then remove the cardboard frames.

Use the pressed fabric as a pattern to cut out a pillow back. Fold the ribbon in half lengthwise and stitch it with a 1/4-inch (6 mm) hem onto the wrong side of the pieced fabric with the folded portion of the ribbon protruding out from the seam. With right sides facing, hand stitch the pillow front to the back, leaving a small opening for turning. Trim the corners, turn right sides out, and press well. Stuff the pillow, then slipstitch the opening closed.

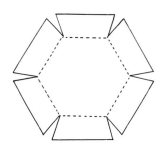

Whole Hexagon Fabric Pattern

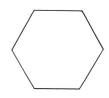

Half Hexagon Fabric Pattern

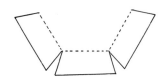

Whole Hexagon Cardboard Pattern

Half Hexagon Cardboard Pattern

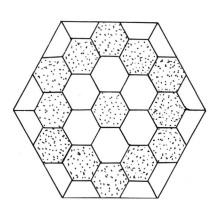

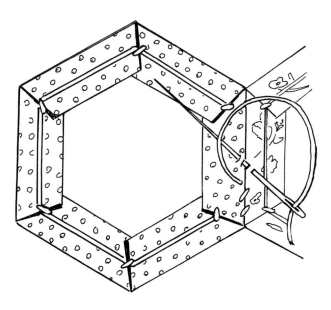

Blooming Pillow

This pincushion pillow owes its lovely sheen to the solid embroidered background. The flower motifs can be used separately or overlapped together to form a larger motif.

MATERIALS

- 6-inch (15 cm) square of cross-stitch cloth with 14 threads per inch
- 4-inch (10 cm) square of ivory linen or cotton
- embroidery floss in the colors called for in the chart
- stuffing

INSTRUCTIONS

Embroider the design in the center of the cloth in a continental tent stitch with undivided strands of floss. (See illustration.) Fill in the background with ivory floss until you have completed a 3-1/4-inch (8 cm) square area with rounded corners.

Trim the fabric 1/2 inch (13 mm) around the embroidery, then cut the 4-inch square of fabric to match the embroidered shape. Sew the two pieces together with right sides facing, taking care that the stitch line runs exactly along the outermost embroidery stitches and leaving a small opening for turning. Trim the seams and turn right sides out. Stuff tightly, then slipstitch the opening closed. To finish, embellish the pillow by twisting two colors of embroidery floss together and tacking them along the outside edge.

Black And White Play

The visual motion in these pillows reveals how deceiving the interplay between black and white can be. Alternative colors of knitting yarn can be substituted, but be sure your colors contrast well.

MATERIALS
FOR EACH PILLOW

- 1 20-inch (50 cm) square of 12-gauge mono canvas
- cotton knitting yarn in black and white
- 20-inch square of black cotton for the pillow back
- stuffing

INSTRUCTIONS

Work the patterns in horizontal satin stitches, referring to the counting diagram as needed. Do all of the black portions first, then go back and fill in the spaces with white.

For the circle motif pillow, work the white satin stitches in vertical columns. For the wavy design, repeat the design until you have a 15-inch (40 cm) square. For both pillows, begin embroidering at the bottom right corners, about 2 inches (5 cm) in from the edge.

With right sides facing, machine stitch the pillow front and back together exactly along the outermost embroidery stitches, leaving an opening for stuffing. Trim the canvas and fabric to a narrow seam allowance and turn right sides out. Stuff the pillow well, then slip-stitch the opening closed with a doubled length of sewing thread.

Each line on the counting diagram represents one fabric thread.

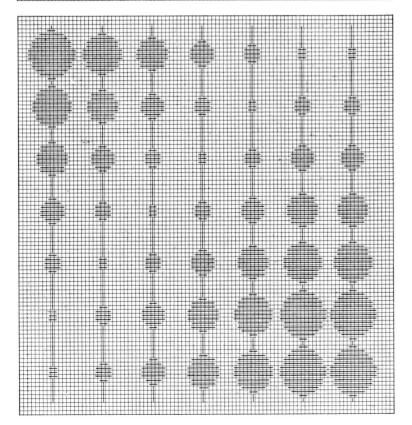

Bird Motif Pincushion

Handling the fine linen fabric and colorful threads as you work on this project is sure to be almost as much fun as using the finished project.

MATERIALS

- 2 5-1/4-inch (13 cm) squares of pink 26-gauge evenweave linen
- colors of embroidery floss indicated in chart
- stuffing
- pink sewing thread

INSTRUCTIONS

Separate the embroidery floss into two-strand lengths and cross-stitch the bird motifs according to the diagram. Press the finished piece facedown on a well-padded ironing board.

Pin the two squares together with right sides facing and sew them shut, leaving a small opening for stuffing. Trim the corners and turn right sides out. Stuff loosely, then slip-stitch the opening closed. To finish, work a border of back stitches in pink sewing thread about 3/8 inch (9 mm) from the outer edge

COLOR CHART

		DMC
T	= Blue	931
$\vee$	= Pale blue	932
$\div$	= Dark green	3346
$\because$	= Light brown	612
$\triangle$	= Light green	3053
$\boxtimes$	= Green	3347
$-$	= Gold green	833

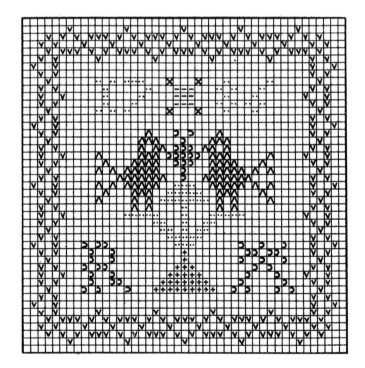

Southwestern Flair

Followers of interior design trends are often appalled at how quickly their "in" looks are labelled "out" and replaced by something newer and more trendy. Fortunately pillows allow you to experiment with new looks without major time or financial investments.

MATERIALS
FOR EACH PILLOW

- 2 18- or 36-inch (46 to 92 cm) squares
- stuffing

INSTRUCTIONS

With right sides facing, stitch all four seams, leaving a small opening for stuffing. Trim the corners and turn right sides out. Stuff the pillow tightly, then slipstitch the opening closed.

Cross-Stitch Scrap Pillow

Made from colorful scraps of leftover floss, this pillow shines with memories from favorite cross-stitch projects.

MATERIALS

- 1 5-inch (12 cm) square of blue cotton, 1 5-inch square of 20-gauge evenweave linen
- scraps of floss
- stuffing

INSTRUCTIONS

Cross-stitch the edges of the linen square, referring to the counting diagram as you work. Work a center square measuring 4-1/2 inches (11 cm) in cross stitches with four strands of floss over two fabric threads. (Note: The plain border will serve as the seam allowance.)

With right sides facing, sew the cross-stitched fabric to the cotton fabric with a 1/2-inch (13 mm) seam allowance, leaving a small opening for turning. Turn right sides out and gently press. Stuff the pillow well, then slip-stitch the opening closed.

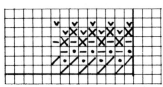

Counting Diagram for Borders/Edges

Colorful Plaids

Add pizazz to your life with these colorful pillows inspired by traditional Scottish plaids. The embroidery is worked in a simple satin stitch.

MATERIALS

FOR EACH PILLOW

- 19-3/4-inch (50 cm) square of embroidery canvas with 11-1/2 mesh per square inch
- 19-3/4-inch square of dark blue fabric
- crewel wool thread in the colors indicated in the color charts
- stuffing

INSTRUCTIONS

Begin embroidering the design in the bottom right portion of your canvas, 2 inches (5 cm) in from the edge, referring to the counting diagram as you work. Each line on the counting diagram represents one thread on the canvas. Work with one strand of wool on your needle, and repeat the design in horizontal and vertical satin stitches until you have a 15-1/2-inch (40 cm) square.

Place the fabric and embroidered canvas together with right sides facing and carefully sew all four seams along the outermost embroidery stitches, leaving an opening for turning. Trim the seams to 3/4-inch (19 mm) and trim the corners diagonally. Turn the pillow right sides out, stuff well, and slip-stitch the opening closed.

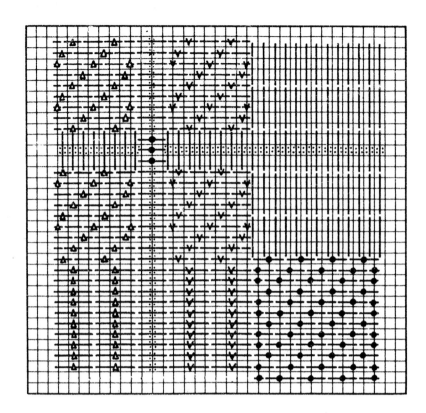

GREEN/BLUE COLOR CHART

		Anchor
● = Black		0403
= Green		0733
△ = Turquoise		0189
= Pale Turquoise		0186
= Blue		0148

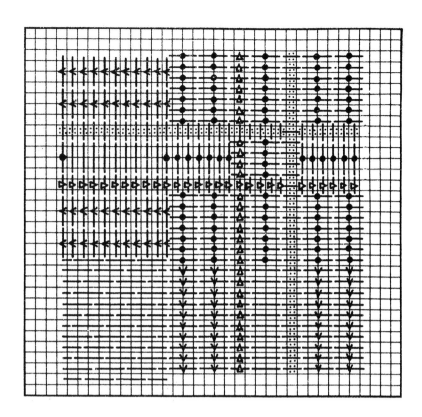

RED/GREEN COLOR CHART

		Anchor
⊞	= Red	019
⊕	= Orange Red	0335
✶	= Turquoise	0189
⠢	= Pale Turquoise	0186
⊞	= Green	0229
⦿	= Blue	0148

PINK/TURQUOISE COLOR CHART

		Anchor
⊟	= Black	0403
⋁	= Green	0189
⠢	= Turquoise	0573
△	= Pale Turquoise	0574
⦿	= Blue	0851

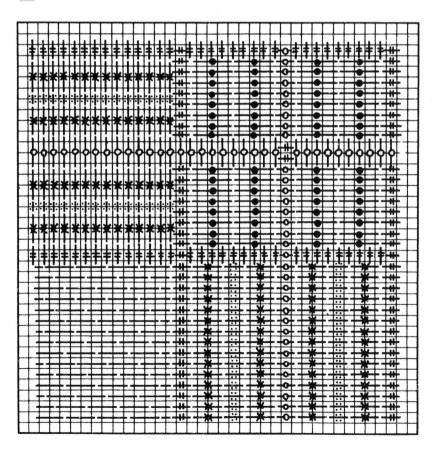

Pincushion Pillow

This delightfully simple pincushion is a fun way to use up extra scraps and takes only minutes to assemble.

MATERIALS

- 2 3-inch (7 cm) fabric squares
- 2/3 yard (.6 m) satin ribbon or bias tape
- fabric glue
- stuffing

INSTRUCTIONS

With right sides facing, sew the two squares together, leaving a narrow opening for stuffing. Trim the seams, turn right sides out, and fill with stuffing. Slipstitch the edges closed.

Cut four lengths of ribbon, two measuring 6-1/2 inches (16 cm) and two measuring 4 inches (10 cm). Mark the centers of all the ribbon lengths with a sewing pin.

Center the middle of one of the longer ribbon lengths at the middle point of the pillow's top side and glue in place. Fold the ribbon ends around the edges and glue around the back side. Repeat the process with the remaining long length of ribbon, this time going in the opposite direction.

Fold each end of the shorter ribbons in to the center mark and glue the edges down. When the glue has completely dried, place one loop on top of the other to form an X. Secure in the center with a few hand-basting stitches and then top-stitch them together in the center. Glue the loops to the pillow top.

Envelope Pillows

As the name implies, this pillow's interesting assembly resembles that of an envelope's. Envelope pillow covers are easily removed, so they're ideal for pillows that require frequent washings.

MATERIALS

- 1-1/2 yards (1.4 m) main fabric
- 1/8 yard (.1 m) contrasting fabric
- 4-inch (10 cm) strip of Velcro
- bed pillow

INSTRUCTIONS
FOR BOTH PILLOWS

Spread the fabric out in a single layer with its right side facing down. Place your pillow on its diagonal in the center of the fabric (see illustration), and trim the fabric to within 1 inch (2.5 cm) of the sides. Your trimmed fabric should be in a square shape.

Fold the two points that will cover the short pillow edges up over the pillow. Measure the distance of each of the unfolded edges, add 4 inches to the measurement, and cut two 2-inch-wide (5 cm) bias strips from the contrasting fabric to this measurement.

Fold the contrasting fabric strips in half lengthwise with right sides facing and press. Apply this trim to the unfolded edges with a 1/2-inch (13 mm) seam. Turn the seam under and continue press-

ing the remaining edges under 1/2 inch. Topstitch 1/4 inch (6 mm) from the folded fabric edge.

Make two 5-inch (12 cm) ties from the contrasting fabric and stitch them to the points of the untrimmed edges. Place the pillow back on top of the fabric and tie the ends together. Fold the trimmed edges up over the pillow one at a time, and mark the area where they overlap with pins. Remove the pillow and sew the Velcro closures in the marked place.

Patchwork Geometrics

A playful approach to geometry makes an interesting way to use up favorite fabric scraps. Feel free to adapt the shapes to suit your fancy.

MATERIALS
FOR EACH PILLOW

- 3/4 yard (.6 m) main fabric
- 3 additional 1/8-yard (.1 m) lengths in complementary colors
- embroidery floss to match fabrics
- wax paper
- stuffing

INSTRUCTIONS
FOR BOTH PILLOWS

Cut out a square slightly larger than you'd like the finished pillow to be from the main fabric and from the wax paper. For pillow 1, divide the wax paper square into four even horizontal strips. For pillow 2, draw diagonal lines from corner to opposite corner. For pillow 3, divide the wax paper into three horizontal strips and then three vertical strips to form nine squares. Cut out the wax paper shapes and add 1/4 inch (6 mm) seam allowance on all seam edges.

For pillow 1, stitch the four long seams and then press open. For pillow 2, stitch pieces A and B together and C and D together. Press the seams open and then stitch pieces AB and CD together on their long edges.

For pillow 3, stitch squares A, B, and C together, then D, E, and F together, and then G, H, and I together. Press all seams open. Sew strip ABC to strip DEF. Next, stitch strips ABC/DEF to strip GHI.

Press all seams open and embellish with a decorative machine or hand embroidery stitch. (See pages 122–124 for illustrated stitches.)

For all pillows, center the pieced square over the backing, trimming them to match if necessary. Finish assembling the pillow, referring to the basic assembly instructions on pages 111 and 112.

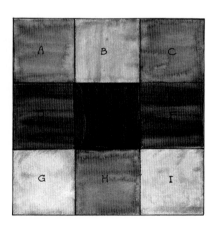

Pillow 1

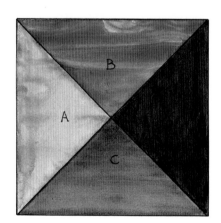

Pillow 2

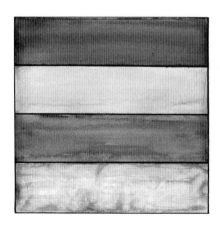

Pillow 3

Surf, Sun, 'N Snooze

Bright pillow shams accented with a sun-shaped pillow add a decorative, nautical flair to any child's room.

MATERIALS
FOR SUN PILLOW

- 1-1/4 yards (1.1 m) main fabric
- 1/4 yard (.2 m) contrasting fabric
- puff paint or embroidery floss
- stuffing

INSTRUCTIONS

Enlarge the pattern 140% and cut out the shape. Use the shape as a pattern to cut out one pillow front from the main fabric. Fold the pattern in half and use it to cut out two backs from the main fabric, adding 1/2 inch (13 mm) for a seam allowance along the folded edge. (See illustration.) Cut out a gusset strip from the main fabric measuring 43 x 3 inches (107 x 7 cm).

For the center appliqué, trace a circle shape from a small plate onto the contrasting fabric. Press the edges down 1/4 inch (6 mm) around all the edges. Add expression to the sun's face with embroidery or puff paint. Pin the decorated face onto the center of the pillow front and topstitch in place.

With right sides facing, stitch the two straight edges of the pillow back, leaving a 4-inch (10 cm) opening in the center for turning and stuffing. Stitch the two gusset ends together with

right sides facing with a 1/2-inch seam. Stitch along the corners of the front and back sun shapes to reinforce the corners.

With right sides facing, pin the sun front to the gusset, taking extra care when pinning the corners. Stitch carefully, and turn right sides out to check for neatness in the corners. Adjust and restitch if necessary, then repeat with the sun back.

Turn the pillow right sides out through the opening and press. Stuff to a medium firmness and stitch the opening closed by hand.

MATERIALS
FOR EACH PILLOW SHAM

- 3 lengths of fabric in contrasting colors measuring 1/3 to 1/2 yard (.3 to .45 m)
- 1-1/2 yards (1.4 m) coordinating color of cording
- 10 sets of metal eyelets wide enough to allow your chosen cording to fit through
- bed pillow

INSTRUCTIONS

Measure the distance around the middle of your pillow with a tape measure and add 2 inches (5 cm). Measure the distance around the long edge of your pillow and add 8 inches (20 cm). From these measurements,

piece a rectangle of fabric from three or four strips of fabric. Feel free to vary the widths of the strips and to sew them together in any order you like.

Fold the fabric in half with right sides facing and stitch the long seam. Turn the sham right sides out. Stitch each of the short ends under with a 1/4-inch (6 mm) and then

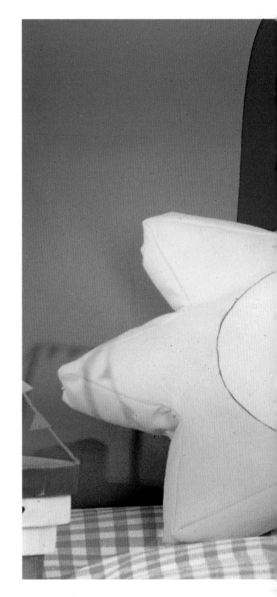

with a 2-inch hem. Press well.

Space five eyelets evenly down each of the short edges about 2 inches in from the folded edge. Apply the eyelets according to the manufacturer's instructions. On the left side of the pillow, lace the cord through the eyelets, tying a knot in each end. Insert the pillow and lace the eyelets as you did for the other side.

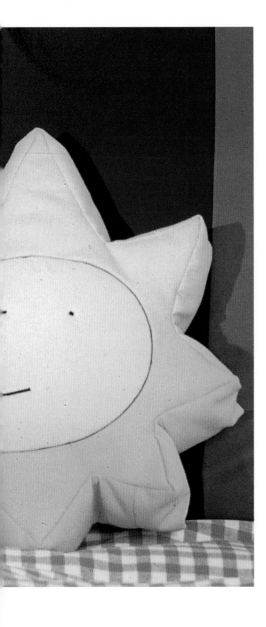

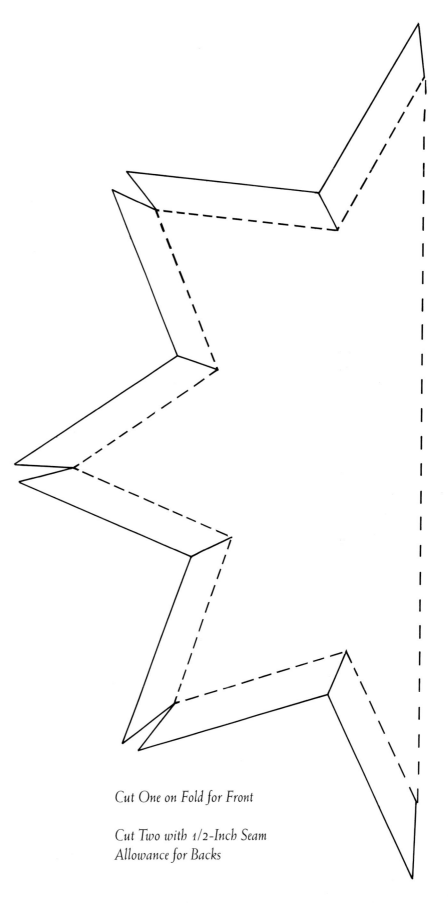

Cut One on Fold for Front

Cut Two with 1/2-Inch Seam Allowance for Backs

Handwoven Pillows

Weavers' studios often offer a selection of sample weaves, many of which are large enough to serve as pillow fronts. Even smaller samples can be used as insets, and you'll soon discover what a wonderful textural dimension handwoven fabrics bring to pillow decorating.

MATERIALS

- 2 squares or rectangles of fabric cut to the identical shape of the woven fabric
- stuffing
- cording (optional)

INSTRUCTIONS

Hand-tack one of the fabric pieces to the wrong side of the woven fabric, folding any uncut threads to the back side of the woven fabric. Place the fabric pillow back against the woven fabric with right sides facing and stitch the seams by hand with a running stitch, leaving a small opening for turning. Turn the pillow right sides out and stuff, then slipstitch the opening closed.

Potpourri Pillow

This charming showcase of needlework skills is filled with a fragrant potpourri. For a couch pillow, just enlarge the embroidery pattern and increase the size of the fabric squares.

MATERIALS

- 2 colors of embroidery floss
- 2 5-inch (12 cm) squares of fabric
- 1-1/4 yards (1.1 m) narrow satin ribbon
- tapestry needle with a large eye and fairly sharp point
- commercial potpourri or fragrant, dried plants from the garden
- disappearing fabric marker

INSTRUCTIONS

Mark off a 3-1/2-inch (8 cm) square in the center of one of the fabric squares. Transfer the design to the fabric. Separate the floss into three-strand lengths and embroider the leaves and flowers with a satin stitch and the stems with a chain stitch.

Place the two fabric squares together with their right sides facing out. Cut four 10-inch (25 cm) lengths of the narrow ribbon. Mark the halfway point of a ribbon length and thread it onto your needle. Adjust the ribbon so that half of it is on your needle and the other half is waiting to be used.

Enter the fabric from the embroidered side on top of the pen guidelines at the middle point. Make one running stitch and return the needle to the top.

continues on following page

continued from previous page

Continue with even running stitches until you reach a corner. Remove the needle but do not cut the ribbon! Go back to the middle point, reinsert the ribbon, and work running stitches until you reach the corner. Again, do not cut the ribbon!

Repeat the above steps on two of the remaining corners. Pour the potpourri or other fragrant material through the opening and then finish embroidering that edge as you did the others. Tie each of the corner ribbons in a bow, then trim the ribbon ends at an angle.

Hand-baste the outer edges of the pillow together about 1/4 inch (6 mm) in from the outer edges. Embroider the edges with a machine- or hand-scalloped buttonhole stitch, then carefully trim off any excess fabric and remove the basting stitches.

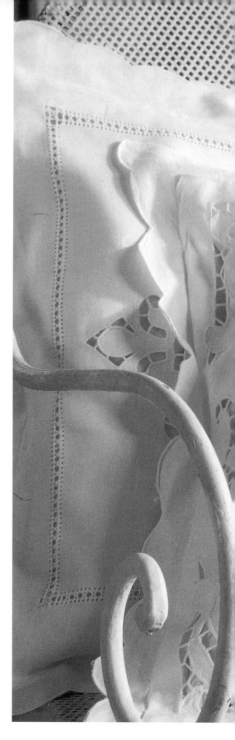

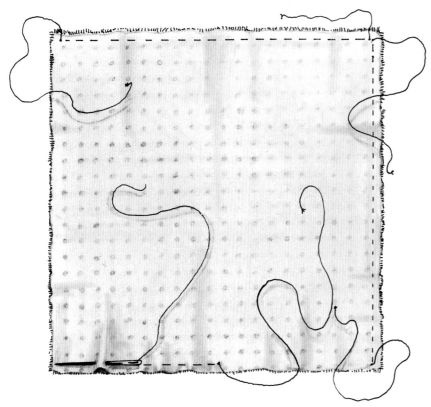

Needle Entry Points

Cutwork Pillow

*Cutwork embroidery has been a beautiful part of lacemaking tradition for hundreds
of years. If you are unfamiliar with cutwork stitching techniques, review and practice
the stitches on page 127 before beginning.*

MATERIALS

- 2/3 yard (.6 m) white linen, white embroidery cotton (weight #s 20 and 25)
- 20-inch square (50 cm) of tracing paper or water-soluble stabilizer
- dressmaker's carbon
- extra-sharp scissors
- 16-1/2-inch square (42 cm) pillow form

INSTRUCTIONS

Cut the linen fabric into one 22-inch (25 cm) square for the pillow front, one 8-5/8- x 17-3/4-inch (21 x 45 cm) rectangle for the lower pillow back, and one 13- x 17-3/4-inch (33 x 45 cm) rectangle for the upper pillow back. Draw a 15-inch (39 cm) square in the center of the tracing paper or stabilizer. Position and trace the center, corner, center side, and center side front motifs onto the tissue paper. Trace the border, repeating the corner/side section at each corner and repeating and connecting the scallops.

Tape the fabric to a piece of cardboard, taking care to keep the grain of the fabric straight.

Line up the corner motifs with the fabric corners. Tape the pattern sheet in place and transfer the motifs to the fabric.

Make two rows of short running stitches on the right side of the fabric along the pattern design with the #25 floss. The first row should be about 1/16 inch (1.5 mm) inside the edge, while the second row should be closer to the edge of the design line. As you stitch the second row, cross each connecting bar with a long stitch (the length of the bar) and return with another long stitch to the first side to continue the short running stitches

Repeat the running stitches on the opposite side of the pattern design. As you stitch the row closest to the design edge, extend a long stitch across the connecting bar and buttonhole stitch back across the 3-thread bar without catching the fabric. The bar should be loose from the fabric, but secured on both ends. Continue the running stitches to the next connecting bar and repeat.

For the branching bars, extend 3 long stitches across the bar, catching a fabric thread at the junction of each branch. Buttonhole stitch back across the 3 long stitches of each branching bar. Repeat for the next branching bar.

Buttonhole stitch the edge of the motifs and the scallop border with #20 floss. The stitches should be 1/16-inch wide and should face the space that will later be cut away. (Use the running stitches as a guideline to ensure even work.) Fill the small circles with a satin stitch and outline the accent lines in the center motif with an outline stitch. When you've completed the embroidery, carefully cut away the spaces to create an openwork effect.

Stitch a 3/8-inch (9 mm) hem on a long side of each of the pillow back pieces. With wrong sides facing and the hems together, pin the two back pieces together to create a square the same size as the pillow front. Place the pinned back section on top of the pillow front with right sides facing and stitch all four edges. Turn right sides out through the overlapped back sections and press well. Insert the pillow form.

CENTER SIDE

15" SQUARE

20" SQUARE

CENTER FRONT

Pillow Basket

For a decorative twist on the common bedside magazine basket, fill an oversized basket with contrasting pillows.

MATERIALS
FOR EACH PILLOW CASING

- fabric, pillow form
- buttons (optional)

INSTRUCTIONS

Cut two lengths of fabric that are 2 inches (5 cm) wider than the dimensions around each direction of the pillow. With right sides facing, stitch the two pieces of fabric together on three of the four seams. Turn right sides out. Press the unsewn seam edge down 1/2 inch (13 mm) and topstitch.

Decide whether to secure the unstitched edge closed with ties or buttons. If ties are desired, cut out six to ten 2- x 10-inch (5 x 25 cm) strips. Fold the strips in half lengthwise with right sides facing and stitch the long seam edge and one of the short edges. Turn right sides out and press. Topstitch the ties in place, positioning the unstitched edges under the topstitching. For a button closure, mark the overlap areas, make buttonholes, and stitch on the buttons.

MATERIALS
FOR RUFFLED PILLOW

- 2 16-inch (41 cm) fabric squares
- 5-yard-length (4.5 m) of 3-inch-wide (7.5 cm) strip for ruffle from contrasting or matching fabric
- stuffing

INSTRUCTIONS

Hem one of the long edges of the ruffle strip and stitch a row of gathering stitches on the other long edge. Gather the ruffle to fit the pillow edge and pin it to the right side of one of the fabric squares. Pin the second square on top of the first with right sides facing. Stitch all four seams, leaving an opening large enough for turning. Trim the seams and turn right sides out. Stuff well, then slipstitch the opening closed.

Crochet Picot Pillow

The handsome picot stitches in this pillow are created from combinations of single and double crochet stitches, chain stitches, and slip stitches. The stitches themselves are simple, but they've been combined in a challenging way. When finished, the crocheted fabric is hand-tacked to the front of a premade pillow.

MATERIALS

- 1 ball DMC Cebelia number 10, size 8 crochet hook (metric size 1.25)
- 15-inch (39 cm) gold fabric pillow
- thick cotton crochet thread

GENERAL INSTRUCTIONS

The stitches used for these projects include the chain stitch (ch), the single crochet stitch (sc), the double crochet stitch (dc), and the slip stitch (sl). Additional abbreviations and symbols used in the instructions include: foll (following, beg (beginning), and * (repeat). Gauge: 12 squares equal 4 inches (10 cm).

INSTRUCTIONS

Make four squares measuring 7-3/4 x 7-3/4 inches (20 x 20 cm). The squares will be joined by the rose at the center. The leaves are worked separately and are sewn on in the finishing steps.

For each square, ch 7, sl st to join in ring. Round 1: Ch 1, work 16 sc in ring, sl st to join in first sc. Round 2: *Ch 5, skip 1 sc and work 1 sc in the foll sc*, rep * to * 7 times = 8 ch-5 arcs. Sl st to join. Round 3: In each arc: 1 sc, 5 dc in 1 sc. Sl st to join in ring. Round 4: *Ch 6 and work 1 sc in the back loop between the changeover of the foll "2 leaves" *, rep * to * around. Sl st to join. Round 5:

In each arc: 1 sc, 6 dc in 1 sc, sl st to join. These leaves come after the leaves of the 3rd round. Round 6: Like round 4.

Round 7: In each arc: 1 sc, 7 dc in 1 sc. Sl st to join. Round 8: This is the beginning of the top background with picots. 1 picot = Ch 4 with 1 sl st in the first ch of these 4 ch's. * **Ch 9, sl 1 in the 6th ch from the hook = 1 picot**, rep ** to ** once, then ch 3 and 1 sc in the changeover between the foll 2 leaves, then for the corner arc: ch 13, sl 1 in the 6th ch from the hook, ch 13, sl 1 in the 6th ch from the hook, ch 7 and 1 sc in the same st like the beg of this corner arc, ch 9, 1 picot = sl 1 in the 4th ch from the hook, ch 9, 1 picot, ch 3, 1 sc in the changeover between the foll 2 leaves*, rep * to * 3 times.

Work 4 corner arcs and work 2 small arcs between them on the sides. Round 9: Sl st to the center of the foll arc, sl st to the back of the picot and work 1 sc in the arc, between the 2 picots, * ** ch 9, 1 picot**, rep ** to ** twice, ch 3, 1 sc in the foll arc between the 2 picots*, rep * to *. Sl to join. Round 10: Sl st to the middle of the foll arc between picots: Work *1 sc, **ch 9, 1 picot**, rep ** to ** twice, ch 3, 1 sc in the sc in the corner arc, work 3 small arcs with 2 picots and 1 sc in

the foll arc 3 times *, rep * to * 3 times. Sl st to join. Round 11: Sl st to center arc and work 1 sc, work in each arc a small arc with 2 picots = 16 arcs. Round 12: Sl st to middle of arc, * in this arc, work 1 corner arc: ch 13, 1 picot, ch 13, 1 picot, ch 7 and work 1 sc in the same arc, work 4 small arcs with 2 picots in the foll arc, work to the foll corner*, rep * to * along the remaining 3 sides.

Round 13: Sl st to center of corner arc and 1 sc. Work 1 round of small arcs with 2 picots = 20 arcs. Round 14: Sl st to middle of foll arc. Work around small arcs and above the corner arc same as round 10 and 1 arc with 1 sc in the sc, the remaining arc with 1 sc in the center of the underlying arc = 24 arcs. Round 15: Sl st to middle of foll arc, 1 sc in the small arcs with 2 picots = 24 arcs, work above each corner 1 arc and along each side 5 arcs. Fasten off.

Make 3 more squares, joining the last round of the 2nd square and the first round of the first square with 1 row of 12 picots as foll: ch 3, sl 1 in the underlying picot, ch 3, 11 sl st in the foll underlying picot, ch 3, 1 sc in the arcs of the underlying row. Work 11 picot in the corner and fasten off. Join all squares as above. The center rose is made by

working the first 7 rounds of the square. Fasten off and sew to center of large square.

For the leaves, ch 10 and wok 7 sc, beg with the 2nd ch from the hook. In the last ch: 3 sc and work 7 sc along the other side of the ch. Ch 3 to turn, working the back loop of the underlying sc , skip the first sc after the turn, in the center sc of the 3 sc, work 3 sc and along the other side, work 7 sc. *Ch 3 to turn, skip 1 sc, work 1 sc across, work 3 sc in the center sc, work 7 sc along the other side*, rep * to * 3 times. Fasten off and make two more leaves.

For the stems, ch 60 with a dou-ble strand of thick cotton cro-chet thread. Join a leaf with a sl st to the 20th and the 50th st. Sc to the 60th ch, turn, then work along the other side in sc. Join the 3rd leaf by sl st to the 30th sc. Fasten off. Flatten the stem and leaves and sew to square as shown in photo. In each corner, make a larger leaf by chaining 14 and work 10 sc instead of 7 sc along each side and work * to * of small leaf 4 times.

To finish, block the pieces to the indicated measurements. Sew the squares together. Around the outside edges, work 1 row of small arcs with 2 picots. Sew a large leaf to each corner, then tack the square to the front of the pillow.

Playtime Brights

The tendency to oversimplify design schemes in children's rooms is often an injustice to everyone involved. The playful mix of prints shown here is easy to replicate, and the large roll pillow provides a hiding place for secret treasures.

MATERIALS
FOR EACH PILLOW

- 2 21-inch squares (52.5 cm) of flannel
- several colors of bright yarn
- tapestry needle
- disappearing fabric marker
- stuffing

INSTRUCTIONS

Arrange and transfer the patterns to the right side of one of your fabric squares. Embroider the designs with the stitches illustrated below. (Refer to the appendix for a review of these stitches if needed.)

Stitch the two squares together with right sides facing, leaving a small opening for turning. Trim the seams and turn right sides out. Measure and mark a 1/2-inch (13 mm) border around the sewn edges. Topstitch over this mark. Stuff the pillow well, then slipstitch the opening closed. Measure and mark a 1/2-inch border out from the slipstitched area and topstitch. Embroider the borders as you like.

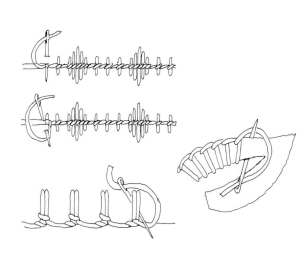

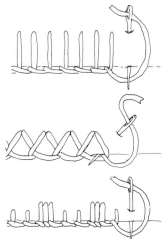

Paneled Pillows

Although these pillows take a little longer to assemble than basic pillow construction, they're well worth the effort if you're working with special fabrics and plan to enjoy the pillows for a long time. Piping and buttons add extra flair to the styling.

MATERIALS
FOR ONE PILLOW

- 1 15-inch (39 cm) square for the back
- 4- x 15-inch (10 x 39 cm) rectangle of fabric for the panel
- one 12- x 15-inch (30 x 39 cm) rectangle of fabric for the front
- 2 yards (1.8 m) contrasting piping (2-1/2 yards (2.2 m) piping for loops if you plan to add optional buttons)
- 8 buttons (optional)

INSTRUCTIONS

Stitch the panel piece to the pillow front. Press the seam toward the front and topstitch 1/8 inch (3 mm) in from the seam line. If you desire piping, pin the piping to one long edge of the panel and then stitch this seam to the front piece. Press the seam toward the front and topstitch 1/8 inch along the front side of the seam. If you desire buttons, form button loops by pinning a length of piping on one end and at even intervals forming loops large enough to go over your buttons. Stitch the seam, press toward the front, and topstitch 1/8 inch away. Stitch the buttons under the loops.

With right sides facing, stitch the front to the back with a 1/2-inch (13 mm) seam, leaving an opening large enough for turning. Turn right sides out and press. Stuff the pillow well, then slipstitch the opening closed.

Embroidered Alphabet

A length of lush burgundy cording and ivory-on-ivory needlework transforms a plain pillow into an elegant showpiece.

MATERIALS

- 1 yard (.9 m) fabric
- 3 yards (2.7 m) decorative cording
- embroidery hoop
- stuffing

INSTRUCTIONS

Mark off a 30- x 18-inch (75 x 46 cm) rectangle on the straight grain of the fabric, but do not cut it out. Transfer the embroidery patterns and put the fabric in the hoop. After embroidering, gently press the wrong side of the fabric. Cut out the rectangle shape.

With right sides facing, stitch all four sides closed, leaving an opening large enough to insert the stuffing. Turn right sides out and stuff the pillow, then slipstitch the opening closed.

Pin the cording with the raw edges of both ends facing each other. Begin pinning one end around the edges. When you hit a corner, allow the cording to protrude over the end about an inch (2.5 cm).

Twist the cording to create a decorative loop, and then continue pinning down the next edge. Repeat until you meet the other end, then slipstitch the cording to the pillow by hand. Readjust the cording where the two ends meet, then trim and stitch down any unraveling threads.

Summer Memories

Curling up with a needlework project is a wonderful way to spend cold winter evenings. The summer motifs ~ butterflies, honeysuckle blooms, and fire thorn berries ~ are beautiful reminders of summer's beauty.

MATERIALS

- 18-inch (46 cm) square of needlework fabric with 25 weave threads per inch
- 18-inch square of cotton in a compatible color
- Danish flower thread and cotton embroidery floss in the colors indicated in the color chart
- stuffing

INSTRUCTIONS

Cross-stitch the motifs as indicated on the chart with two strands of thread. Work the back stitches in one strand of thread. The back stitches in and around the flowers should be done in Deep Pink; the back stitches in and around the leaves should be done in dark green; and the back stitches done in and around the butterflies should be done in brown.

Press the finished fabric facedown on a padded surface. With right sides facing, stitch the four pillow seams, leaving a small opening for stuffing. To prevent unraveling, stitch a row of zigzag stitches on the outer edge of the first seam. Trim the seams and turn right sides out. Stuff the pillow tightly, then slipstitch the opening closed.

COLOR CHART FOR DANISH FLOWER THREAD

■	= Dark Green	210
●	= Green	9
::	= Pale Green	231
▼	= Deep Purple (Eggplant)	4
⊠	= Red	86
⟋	= Pink	503
‒	= Pale Pink	12
⌐	= Pale Yellow	31
⌐	= Very Pale Yellow	225

COLOR CHART FOR D.M.C.

		DMC
◣	= Black	310
▼	= Brown	611
⋁	= Light Brown	3046
.·	= Ivory	3047
·	= White	White
○	= Yellow	743
Z	= Dark Yellow	972

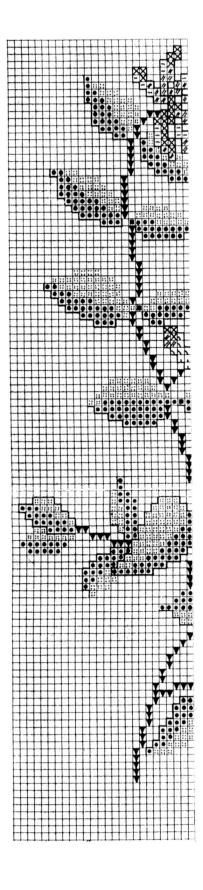

Gold Pillows

Machine quilting has become a popular alternative to the time-consuming hand method and is especially handsome when used to embellish solid blocks of fabric.

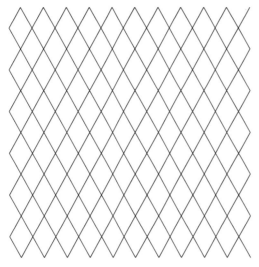

MATERIALS
FOR EACH PILLOW

- 3 20-inch (50 cm) squares of fabric (one of the squares will not be seen in the finished project and can be any material with compatible laundering needs)

- 1 20-inch square of quilt batting

- stuffing

- transparent nylon or gold quilting thread

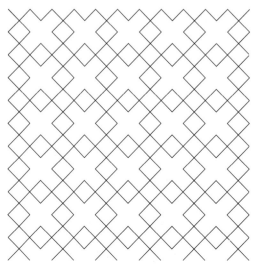

INSTRUCTIONS

Make a quilting sandwich with a fabric square on the bottom (this square will not be seen in the finished pillow), the batting in the middle, and one of the gold squares on top with its right side facing up. Hand-baste the layers together with a diagonal X from corner to corner. On an enlarging photocopying machine increase the size of your favorite quilting pattern to a size you like and transfer it to the right side of the fabric. Machine quilt over your transfer markings. Finish assembling the pillow, referring to the basic assembly guidelines on pages 11 and 12 if needed.

Appliqué Blooms

Appliqué motifs are the perfect use for small scraps of cotton prints, and today's iron-on fabric adhesives allow you to complete projects quickly with superb quality.

MATERIALS

- small scraps of cotton in four different prints
- 1/3 yard (.3m) of a fifth print for the flower and binding
- iron-on adhesive
- stuffing
- 1/2 yard (.45 m) solid color fabric

INSTRUCTIONS

Cut bias strips for the cording from the 1/3-yard piece of fabric. Save any remaining scraps for the flower motif. Photocopy the pattern and cut out the pieces. Study the layout of the pattern and experiment with fabric choices until you're happy with the results.

Iron the adhesive onto the wrong sides of the fabric scraps, then pin the pattern pieces onto the fabric and cut through both layers. Peel off the adhesive and iron the pieces in place on the main fabric. Note: The designer for the pillow shown here chose to place the motif in the bottom left corner. Other options include centering the design in the middle of the pillow or repeating it in all four corners.

Finish the appliqué by zigzagging around the edges of each piece with a narrow stitch setting. Fold the bias strips into a cord and complete the pillow, referring to the basic instruction on pages 11–13 if needed.

Braided Smocking

The Japanese smocking technique used for these pillows creates a lovely wicker pattern. The pillows are shown in two variations, one with a pleated edge and the other with a gathered edge.

MATERIALS
FOR ONE PILLOW

- 1-1/2-yard (1.4 m) 60-inch-wide (150 cm) striped fabric
- 16-inch (41 cm) filler pillow

INSTRUCTIONS
FOR EITHER PILLOW

Cut a 31-1/2-inch (80 cm) square for the pillow front and two 10-5/8- x 16-5/8-inch (26 x 42 cm) rectangles for the back. Spread the remaining fabric out flat with its right side facing down. For the pleated-edge pillow, draw a 20-5/8-inch (52 cm) square in the center of the fabric in pencil. For the gathered-edge pillow, draw a 24-3/4-inch (61 cm) square in the center of the fabric in pencil.

Inside the squares, draw rows of vertical and horizontal dots in 1-3/8-inch (3.5 cm) intervals. Beginning in the bottom right-hand corner, draw more dots around the square outline at 2-3/4-inch (6 cm) intervals. These dots will be used to indicate the smocking patterns.

Study the drawing carefully. Begin working at Point 1 and continue working through Point 5, which will equal point 1 again. Hold the fabric so that the stripes run vertically. Begin at the bottom right and work in vertical rows. Fasten the thread in the corner point.

Stick the needle in diagonally to Point 2, then pull the thread to form a pleat. Make several back stitches to secure the thread. Now insert the needle horizontally to the left to Point 3 and again fasten the thread to secure. Cross over to Point 4, pull the thread to form another pleat, and fasten the thread. Insert the needle horizontally to the right at Point 5 and fasten the thread again.

Continue in this way until you have done all the vertical dots, then go on to the following rows until you've finished. For the pleated-edge pillow, there will be a narrow row of dots left over on the left side. Keep sewing the two diagonal dots, Points 1 and 2, to each other, then make a cross-over stitch to Point 5. Create the pleated edge by basting in 8 pleats on each side of the pillow, trying to keep their height and spacing as close to the smocked pleats as possible. Double check that the smocked work is centered, then cut the fabric to a 16-5/8-inch square.

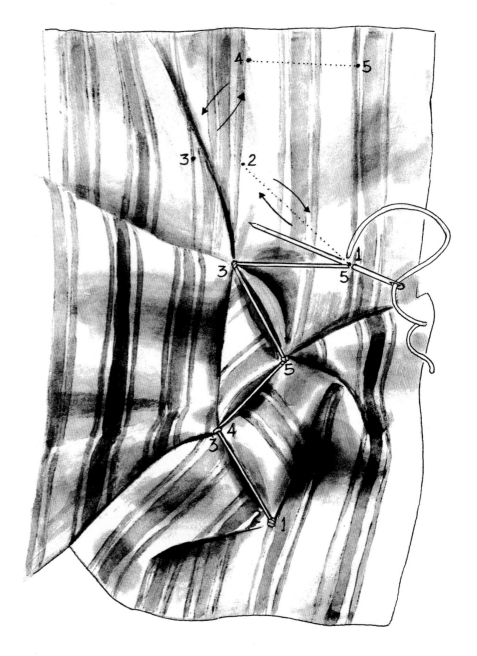

Sew a loose gathering stitch about 1-1/2 inch (4 cm) out from the smocking around the outside edges. Gather until you have a 15-3/4-inch square, then trim a 3/8-inch (9 mm) allowance outside the gathered edge.

Sew a narrow hem on one of the long sides of both pillow backing pieces. Overlap the two pieces on top of each other with their right sides facing up to form a 16-5/8-inch square. Sew the front and back of the pillow together with right sides facing and turn right sides out through the overlapped back. Insert the filler pillow.

Custom Fabric Pillows

Surface design has become an increasingly alluring field for fiber artists, much to the benefit of fabric consumers looking for unique decorating materials. Although these custom-made fabrics tend to be more costly than mass-produced fabrics, you don't need much fabric for a simple pillow.

MATERIALS
FOR EACH PILLOW

- 2 20-inch squares (50 cm) of fabric
- contrasting cording (optional)
- stuffing

INSTRUCTIONS

Pin the squares together with right sides facing and stitch all four sides, leaving an opening large enough for turning. Trim the seams and turn right sides out. Stuff pillow well, then slip-stitch the opening closed.

Cross-Stitched Hydrangea

The beauty of cross-stitch and patchwork combine to create a lovely showpiece of handwork.

MATERIALS

- 1/2 yard (.45 m) cross-stitch fabric
- 3/4 yard (.6 m) border and backing fabric
- embroidery flosses as indicated in chart
- stuffing

INSTRUCTIONS

Cross-stitch the hydrangea design according to the chart. Trim the cross-stitched fabric to a 14-1/4-inch (37 cm) square. Cut 4 2-1/4- x 18-inch (10 x 46 cm) border strips. Assemble a mitered border, referring to the basic instructions on page 15 if necessary.

Cut a 16-inch (41 cm) square for the pillow back. With right sides together, stitch all four seams, leaving a small opening for stuffing. Trim the seams and turn right sides out. Stuff the pillow tightly, then slipstitch the opening closed.

KEY TO CHART

		DMC	Anchor			DMC	Anchor			DMC	Anchor
·	= White	2	white	■	= Medium ocean blue	122	792	▲	= Medium dark pine	217	501
●	= Light grape	117	341	/	= Light jade	213	504	⌐	= Lavender	342	211
●	= Grape	118	340	−	= Light lime	214	369	∨	= Light pine	875	503
		= Light ocean blue	120	794	+	= Medium jade	215	368	●	= Medium pine	877	502

Filet Crochet Pillows

Filet crochet, which enjoyed the height of its popularity several hundred years ago, is enjoying a surge of interest as crocheters rediscover the lacelike filet motifs that can be made from simple stitches. If you've never crocheted a filet pattern before, please refer to the appendix for a basic review of the stitches and techniques.

MATERIALS

FOR EACH PILLOW

- 2 50-gram balls of white Mayflower cotton 8
- crochet hook B/1 (metric size 2.5)
- 13-inch (33 cm) pillow form for the heart motif pillow
- 14-inch (36 cm) pillow form for the peacock motif pillow

GENERAL INSTRUCTIONS

The stitches used for these projects include the chain stitch (ch), the single crochet stitch (sc), the double crochet stitch (dc), and the slip stitch (sl). Additional abbreviations and symbols used in the instructions include: foll (following), beg (beginning), and * (repeat). Gauge: 12 squares equal 4 inches (10 cm).

Each open square in the motif chart equals 1 chain and 1 double crochet. The last double crochet of each square is the first double crochet of the following square. Each filled square equals 2 double crochets plus the last double crochet of the previous square. Work by following the squares in the chart: 1 cross on the chart is a filled square and an open square on the chart equals an open square. To make the reverse pillows, reverse the chart.

Note to British Crocheters: Slip stitch equals single crochet; single crochet equals double crochet; double crochet equals treble crochet.

INSTRUCTIONS

FOR THE PEACOCK DESIGN WITH FILLED SQUARES:

Ch 79 + ch 4 = first open square. Row 1: Work the foll dc in the 7th ch from the hook. Now work in open squares: *ch 1, skip 1 ch, 1 dc in the foll ch*, rep * to * 37 times = 39 open squares. Row 2: Ch 4 for the first open square, 1 dc in the foll dc, *ch 1, 1 dc in the foll dc*, rep * to *. Work 3 rows same as the second row.

Continue by foll chart, beg with 10 open squares, 2 filled squares, 1 dc in the underlying ch, 1 dc in the foll dc, 1 dc in the foll underlying ch, 1 dc in the foll dc, then 1 dc in the foll dc, then 1 open square, 1 filled square, 1 open square, 1 filled square, 1 open square, 1 filled square and work to end in open squares. Continue by foll chart.

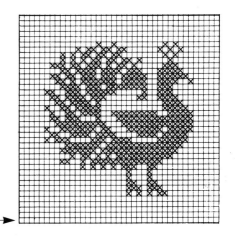

1st row →

⊠ = Filled square

☐ = open square

COLOR CHART

		DMC	Anchor			DMC	Anchor
−	= Blue	793	0147	‖	= Yellow	726	0295
●	= Dark Red	902	0430	+	= Orange Brown	921	
o	= Rust Brown	347	0412	‖	= Purple	315	
	= Orange	970	0332	/	= Mauve	3042	
∨	= Green	910	0737	.	= Ivory	543	
⊠	= Black	310	0403				

MATERIALS

- 18- x 22-inch (46 x 55 cm) rectangle of white linen with 13 weave threads per inch
- 16- x 20-inch (41 x 50 cm) rectangle of white linen
- crewel wool thread in the colors listed in the chart
- stuffing

INSTRUCTIONS

Embroider the center design in satin stitch with one strand of wool, following the counting diagram. Count 11 fabric weave threads out from the center design and embroider a frame of diagonally worked back stitches with one strand of black wool.

Cut the finished embroidered fabric into a 16- x 20-inch rectangle. Gently press the wrong side of the embroidery on a well-padded surface. Make four multicolored tassels and pin them to the right side of the embroidered fabric in the corners. Place the second rectangle against the first with right sides facing. Sew all four seams, leaving a small opening for stuffing. Turn right sides out. Stuff the pillow tightly, then slipstitch the opening closed.

Making Tassels

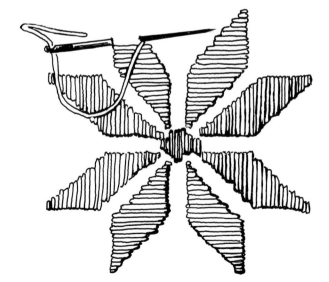

INSTRUCTIONS
FOR TASSEL

Cut out a 1- x 4-inch (2.5 x 10 cm) piece of cardboard and wind embroidery floss or yarn around it. (Note: The size of the cardboard can be increased or decreased to change the size of your finished tassel.) Loop through a piece of yarn at the top and tie a knot. Cut the bottom loops open. Tie a thread around the tassel about 1/2 inch (13 mm) down from the top, then cut the tassel to the right length.

Patchwork Pleasures

These patchwork pillows are the perfect way to use up small scraps of fabric. Don't waste time trying to make them all identical; part of their charm comes from their random pattern assembly.

MATERIALS

- scraps of five to eight different fabrics
- 19-inch (48 cm) square of fabric for the pillow back
- stuffing

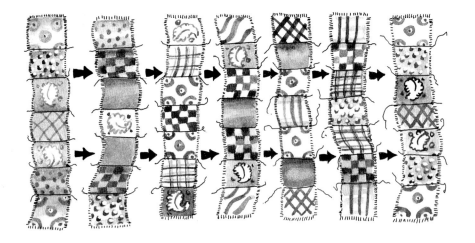

INSTRUCTIONS

Cut out 49 3-inch (7.5 cm) squares for piecing the center of the pillow and 4 3-inch squares for the corners. Next, cut 4 strips measuring 3 inches x 15 inches (7.5 x 39 cm) for the sides.

Arrange and pin the 3-inch squares into seven strips that each have seven squares in them. Sew the seams with a 1/2-inch (13 mm) seam allowance, then press all the seams open. Pin and stitch the seven strips together, taking care that the horizontal seams match. Press all the seams open.

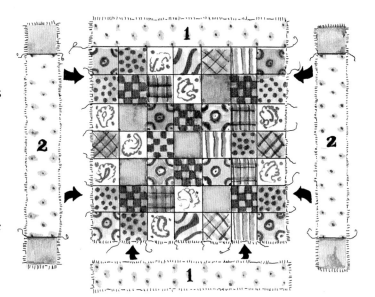

Pin and stitch a side strip to the top and bottom of the large pieced square. Press the seams open. Stitch a 3-inch square to each end of the remaining two strips and press well. Pin the strips to the unbordered sides, again taking care to line up the seams. Press well.

With right sides facing, stitch the pieced pillow front to the pillow back, leaving a small opening for turning. Turn the pillow right sides out and press well. Stuff the pillow, then slipstitch the opening closed.

Design Echoes

Replicating the same pattern on two pillows with two differ-ent techniques makes the perfect project for crafters who are easily bored. Additional pillows can be made along the same theme, using applique, embroidery, and tufting techniques.

MATERIALS
FOR QUILTED PILLOW

- 3 20-inch (50 cm) squares of fabric and 1 of batting
- 1 yard (.9 m) contrasting cording
- disappearing fabric pen
- embroidery floss and needle
- foam pillow insert or stuffing

MATERIALS
FOR PAINTED PILLOW

- 2 20-inch squares of fabric
- 1 yard contrasting cording
- disappearing fabric pen
- embroidery floss and/or fabric paint and small craft paintbrush
- foam pillow insert or stuffing

INSTRUCTIONS
FOR BOTH PILLOWS

Photocopy four copies of the pattern and cut out the motifs. Play with positioning them in all four corners until you're happy with their look. Pin them in place and trace the outlines with the disappearing fabric pen. Remove the patterns.

For the quilted pillow, baste the batting to the wrong side of one of the fabric squares. Quilt over the fabric-pen lines with a long running stitch, then repeat 1/8 inch (3 mm) on the inside of the first line. Trim the batting edges just a little larger than your seam allowance.

For the painted pillow, squirt some fabric paint onto a stack of newspaper. Begin painting, working on the motif closest to you and turning the square around as you work. Note: You may wish to dilute some of the paint with water to create a shadowed effect.

For both pillows, add the cording and finish the pillows, referring to the basic instruction on pages 11 through 13 if necessary.

Quick Pillows

*Try these lively pillows for an energizing burst
of color that takes only minutes to create.*

MATERIALS
FOR EACH PILLOW

- 2 16-inch (40 cm) fabric squares in contrasting colors
- disappearing fabric marker, 15-inch strip (38 cm) of Velcro (optional)
- 15-inch pillow form

INSTRUCTIONS

Zigzag the outer edges of each square with a wide stitch in a thread color that contrasts well with the fabric. On the right side of the fabric, mark a border 1 inch (2.5 cm) around the outer edges with the disappearing marker. Pin the two squares together with wrong sides facing and stitch over the border markings on three of the four edges. Insert the pillow, then secure the fourth edge shut with a strip of Velcro or top stitching.

Day Bed Pillows

An interesting collection of pillow shapes in soft cotton prints transforms a daybed into an oasis of relaxation.

MATERIALS
FOR EACH THROW PILLOW

- 1/2 to 1 yard (.45 to .9 m) stripe or plaid print for each pillow
- stuffing

Cut the fabric into two identical squares or rectangles. (12 to 16 inches, 30 to 41 cm, makes a nice square pillow and 18 x 36 inches, 46 x 92 cm, makes a good rectangular pillow.) With right sides facing, stitch all four sides, leaving an opening large enough to insert the stuffing. Turn right sides out and stuff well, then slipstitch the opening closed.

MATERIALS
FOR CUSHION PILLOW

- 1 yard (.9 m) length of wide ribbon
- 3 - 4 yards (2.7 - 3.6 m) striped fabric (precise fabric requirements will depend on your bed's size)
- stuffing

INSTRUCTIONS

Decide if you'd like the pillow cushion to go around all three sides of the bed or just two. (See photo.) Measure the distance that you'd like to cover and add 2-1/2 inches (6 cm). Cut the fabric to this length. For the width, measure out 16 inches (41 cm) from the fold mark and trim off the excess fabric. Note: The excess fabric makes a nice inset piece for a comforter.

Refold the fabric with right sides facing and stitch the long seam and one of the short seams. Turn right sides out and press. Fold down the edges of the unstitched side 1/4 inch (6 mm) and topstitch, then fold down another 2 inches (5 cm) and press. Stuff the pillow tube loosely enough to allow it to curve around the corners. Tie the open end closed with the ribbon about 3 inches (7.5 cm) down from the folded edge.

Creature
Comforts

Lounge Pillow

Comfortable outdoor furniture allows you to enjoy your gardening efforts.

MATERIALS

- 1/2 yard (.45 m) fabric
- stuffing
- 3 yards (2.7 m) bias cording

INSTRUCTIONS

Cut out two rectangles, using the width of your chair plus 1 inch (2.5 cm) for the width and 16 inches (41 cm) for the depth. Cut two 48-inch (120 cm) lengths from the bias cording and fold them in half. Pin the two rectangles together with right sides facing. Insert the cording loop into the top corner seam allowance and pin securely. Stitch the pieces together, leaving an opening large enough to insert the stuffing. Turn right sides out and stuff tightly, then slipstitch the opening closed.

Bench Pillows

Who says home decorating has to be limited to the inside of your home? These wide-striped pillows tie the garden pots and furniture together for a great garden look.

MATERIALS
FOR TWO PILLOWS

- 2-1/2 yards (2.25 m) striped fabric (may be slightly more or less, depending on your bench's size)
- stuffing

INSTRUCTIONS

Measure the distance of your bench's back. Add 1 inch (2.5 cm) on all sides, and then cut out four squares of fabric to this measurement. Pin the squares together with right sides facing. Sew all four seams, leaving a small opening for stuffing. Turn right sides out and stuff the pillows, then slip-stitch the opening closed.

Blue Hues

Simple pillows in a variety of floral, plaid, and striped prints create an inviting warmth and depth to contemporary upholstery. If you avoid the temptation to add decorative cording or ruffles, the pillows can easily be started and finished in an evening.

MATERIALS
FOR EACH PILLOW

- 2 16-inch (41 cm) fabric squares
- stuffing

INSTRUCTIONS

With right sides facing, stitch all four seams, leaving a small opening for stuffing. Turn right sides out and stuff the pillow tightly, then slipstitch the opening closed.

Nursery Pillows

Small pillows are always a welcome baby gift, and those embellished with handwork make cherished keepsakes. Small muslin bags of dried lavender or mint can be added with the pillow stuffing to add a light fragrance to baby's room.

MATERIALS
FOR EACH PILLOW

- 2 12-inch (30 cm) squares of fabric
- embroidery hoop
- embroidery floss and needle
- stuffing

INSTRUCTIONS

Hand-baste one of the fabric squares to a piece of fabric large enough to allow the square's corner areas to fit in the embroidery hoop, and transfer the embroidery pattern. For the ABC and flower motif pillows, work the pattern in a chain or stem stitch using three strands of floss. For the inter-locking chain pillow, work the pattern in a whipped running stitch with six strands of floss.

Press the embroidered fabric. Pin the two fabric squares right sides together and sew, leaving an opening large enough to insert the stuffing. Turn right sides out and stuff the pillow, then slipstitch the opening closed.

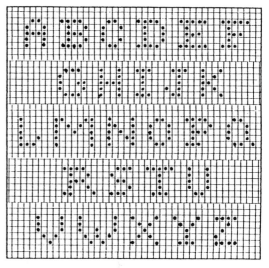

Sweet Dreams

This charming version of the traditional sleep pillow is embroidered with a simple satin stitch. For a larger pillow, consider using crewel threads.

MATERIALS

- 2 16- x 12-inch (41 x 27 cm) rectangles
- 1-1/2 yards (1.35 m) of 3-inch-wide (7.5 cm) contrasting fabric for ruffle
- embroidery floss

INSTRUCTIONS

Transfer the motif to the right side of one of the rectangles. Embroider the letters in a satin stitch, then press the fabric from the wrong side. Hem one of the long ends of the ruffle fabric and gather the other long end to fit around the right side of the pillow front. Pin the pillow back to the front with right sides facing and stitch all four seams, leaving an opening large enough for turning. Turn right sides out, stuff well, and slipstitch the opening closed.

Playtime Checks

Pillows made from bright gingham checks and fun motif prints make a playful grouping for a young person's room.

MATERIALS
FOR EACH PILLOW

- cotton print fabric (amount will vary depending on your pillow's size)
- pillow
- disappearing fabric marker

INSTRUCTIONS

Measure the distance around the long and short ends of a pillow. Add 3 inches (7.5 cm) to each measurement and cut out two pieces of fabric to these dimensions. With right sides facing, pin and stitch both short ends and one long end. Stitch about 2 inches (5 cm) of the long seam from each edge on the remaining long seam. Turn right sides out and press. Measure and mark a line 2 inches in from the outside of all the sewn corners. Stitch over the marked line. Insert the pillow and slip-stitch the opening closed. Measure and mark a line 2 inches in from the slipstitched edge and machine stitch, taking care not to stitch over the pillow.

Pillow Shams

A closet full of colorful pillow shams makes a fun and inexpensive way to change your bedroom's design every time you change the sheets.

MATERIALS
FOR ONE PILLOW

- standard bedroom pillow
- 1-1/2 yards (1.35 m) fabric

INSTRUCTIONS

Cut one rectangle of fabric measuring 24 x 34 inches (60 x 85 cm) for the front, one rectangle of fabric measuring 24 x 30 inches (60 x 75 cm) for the lower back, and one rectangle of fabric measuring 24 x 8 inches (60 x 20 cm).

Turn under and stitch a 1/4-inch (6 mm) hem along one of the short sides of the lower back piece. Finish one 24-inch edge of the upper back piece. Fold and press a 2-inch (5 cm) hem along this same edge. Overlap the hem of the upper back piece 2 inches over the finished edge of the lower back piece. Baste the side edges together. The overall finished length should be 34 inches at this point.

With right sides together, stitch the front and back together with a 1/2-inch (3 mm) seam. Turn and press. With right sides facing outward, measure and pin a line 1-1/2 inch (4 cm) in from the finished edge. Top-stitch along this line to create a flat border around the pillow. Insert the pillow.

MATERIALS
FOR TIE PILLOW

- standard bedroom pillow
- 1-1/2 yards (1.35 m) fabric

INSTRUCTIONS

From the main fabric, cut two rectangles measuring 21 x 31 inches (52 x 77 cm) and two tie ends measuring 4 x 7 inches (10 x 17 cm). Cut two facings measuring 21 x 4 inches (52 x 10 cm) from the contrast material.

Fold each tie end piece in half lengthwise and stitch the edges with a 1/2-inch (13 mm) seam, leaving one end open. Turn and press. Center and pin the tie ends on the 21-inch edge of the right side of each sham half.

Place the tie end in the center of the right side of the rectangle. Pin the facing piece to the rectangle with right sides facing, double checking to be sure that the tie end has been caught in the seam. Stitch the seam. Repeat with the second rectangle and press. (See illustrations.) With right sides facing, stitch the side and bottom seams. Turn and press.

Fold the facing in to meet the facing seam and hand or machine stitch to the seam to secure. Insert the pillow through one of the sides and tie the ties.

Delightful Details

It's often a simple detail that makes the subtle difference between an ordinary pillow and a special one. Here, simple pillow constructions have been dressed up with contrasting cording.

MATERIALS
FOR EACH RUFFLED PILLOW

- 2 20-inch (50 cm) fabric squares
- 1/3 yard (.3 m) matching or contrasting fabric for ruffle
- 3 yards (2.7 m) matching or contrasting cording
- stuffing

MATERIALS
FOR EACH UNRUFFLED PILLOW

- 2 20-inch fabric squares
- 3 yards matching or contrasting cording
- stuffing

INSTRUCTIONS

For the ruffled pillow, cut and piece a 3-inch-wide (7.5 cm) length of fabric into a 13-yard (11.7 m) length. Stitch a row of gathering stitches on one long end and a narrow hem on the other long end. Gather the ruffle until it fits the outside seam edges of the pillow. Pin the cording to the right side of one of the fabric squares, then pin the ruffle on top of it. Place the second fabric square on top of the first with right sides facing and stitch all four seams, leaving a small opening for turning. Turn right sides out, stuff, and slipstitch the opening closed.

For the unruffled pillow, pin the cording around the right side of one of the fabric squares. Pin the second square on top of the first with right sides facing. Stitch all four seams, leaving a small opening for turning. Turn right sides out, stuff, and slipstitch the opening closed.

Drawn Thread Work

Drawn thread is generally worked by removing or maneuvering select threads from a length of fabric and then securing and embellishing the threads with embroidery stitches. If you're not familiar with the basic techniques of drawn thread work, review the instructions on page 126 and practice using the chart before you begin.

MATERIALS

- 2/3 yard (.6 m) ivory linen with a thread count of 20 stitches per inch (2.5 cm)
- linen or linen-blend embroidery thread in a light grey or matching ivory
- stuffing

INSTRUCTIONS

Referring to the chart as you work, embroider 16 full designs for the center of the pillow. Embroider 16 half designs to create the border and then a quarter design in each corner. Each design is created through a combination of the star stitch, the flat stitch, and the closet stitch. Each line in the chart represents one thread. The star stitches at the edges of each design serve as connectors, so embroider them only once.

Secure the edges as reviewed in the appendix. Trim the embroidered fabric into a square with a 1/2-inch (13 mm) seam allowance and then cut an identical piece for the pillow back. With right sides facing, stitch all four seams, leaving a small opening for stuffing. Trim the corner seams and turn right sides out. Stuff the pillow tightly, then slipstitch the opening closed.

left to right: star stitch, flat stitch, closet stitch

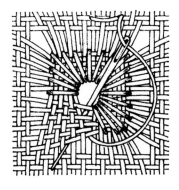
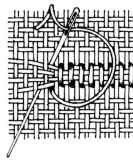
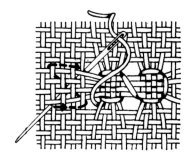

Ivory Complements

The elegance of white and ivory upholstery can become a little mundane after a while, but a stack of pillows in assorted upholstery prints adds instant life.

MATERIALS
FOR EACH PILLOW
- 2 18-inch (46 cm) upholstery fabric squares
- stuffing

INSTRUCTIONS
With right sides facing, stitch all four seams, leaving a small opening for stuffing. Trim the seams and turn the pillow right sides out. Stuff the pillow tightly, then slipstitch the opening closed.

Bow Pillows

Bows can be used to dress up a simple pillow, or, as shown in the pillows here, they can tie together a combination of prints. For the holidays, consider tying strips of holiday fabric around your existing pillows for a quick, festive look.

MATERIALS
FOR EACH PILLOW

- 1/2 yard (.45 m) main fabric
- 1/2 yard contrasting fabric
- stuffing

INSTRUCTIONS

Cut out two 16-inch (41 cm) squares and sew them together with right sides facing, leaving a small opening for stuffing. Trim the corner seams and turn right side out. Stuff tightly, then slip-stitch the opening closed.

For the ties, cut two strips measuring 6 inches (15 cm) wide and 60 inches (150 cm) long. Fold each strip in half with right sides facing. Sew the long seam and one of the short seams. Trim the seams and turn right sides out. Press the strips well, arranging the seam lines so they run down the center back of the strips. Mark the halfway points of both strips and tack them to the center of the pillow back. Loosely bring the strips around the pillow to the center front and tie in a bow.

Style Blends

Medallions of classic cross-stitched Victorian roses with contemporary embroidered borders work together to create these pillows of timeless design.

INSTRUCTIONS
FOR BOTH PILLOWS

Separate the flosses into three-strand lengths and work the patterns as indicated in the charts. Block the back side of the finished needlework with a hot iron. Cut out a square from the needleworked fabric, allowing for seam allowance and border if desired, then cut out a second piece of fabric for the backing. Assemble the pillows, referring to the basic instructions on pages 11 and 12 if necessary.

MATERIALS
FOR BRITTANY STRIPES PILLOW SHOWN ON PAGE 108

- 1/2 yard (.45 m) neutral color of linen
- embroidery flosses listed in chart
- needle
- stuffing

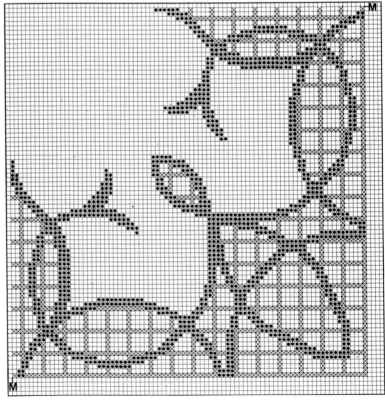

MATERIALS

FOR TRELLIS BORDER PILLOW
SHOWN ON PAGE 109

- 1/2 yard neutral color of linen
- embroidery flosses listed in chart
- needle
- stuffing

Trim Treats

Decorative trims transform even the most boring of pillows into playful design expressions. Wedding and birth dates can be added with embroidery to create custom gift pillows.

MATERIALS
FOR EACH PILLOW

- 2 18-inch (46 cm) squares of fabric
- 3 yards (2.7 m) eyelet edging for the ruffle
- assortment of decorative ribbons and lace trims
- disappearing fabric marker
- stuffing

INSTRUCTIONS
FOR BOTH PILLOWS

Trace a large heart, square, or rectangular shape onto the right side of one of the squares. (Other motifs, such as favorite animals or flowers, can be substituted.) Pin a length of ribbon or lace over the shape, then follow with several additional rows inside the first. Topstitch the trims in place with matching thread, then press well.

Stitch a row of gathering stitches to the unfinished edge of the eyelet. Gather to fit the pillow and pin to the inside edge of one of the squares with right sides facing. Place the remaining square on top with right sides facing and pin. Stitch all four sides, leaving a small opening for stuffing. Trim the corner seams and turn right sides out. Stuff the pillow tightly and then slipstitch the opening closed.

Print Blends

Although they may seem incongruous, pillows made from floral and plaid prints can look great together, especially if the colors are of the same hue. Adding a few solid-color pillows polishes the look.

MATERIALS
FOR EACH PILLOW

- 2 16-inch (41 cm) fabric squares
- stuffing

INSTRUCTIONS

With right sides facing, stitch all four seams, leaving a small opening for stuffing. Turn right sides out and stuff the pillow tightly, then slip-stitch the opening closed.

Outdoor Comfort

Twig furniture looks great outdoors, but for long-term sitting it can be outright uncomfortable. These pillows provide comfort as well as color and can be made from virtually any fabric.

MATERIALS
FOR EACH SITTING CUSHION

- 2-inch-thick (5 cm) foam cushion in a size and shape to fit your sitting area
- sturdy fabric
- newspaper
- matching zipper long enough to fit the back side of the foam cushion

INSTRUCTIONS

Measure the distances around both directions of the foam cushion. Cut out a rectangle from these dimensions from the newspaper, adding 1/2 inch (13 mm) to all sides for the seam allowance. For the side gusset pieces, measure the length and height of the sides. Add 1/2 inch to all sides and cut out 2 newspaper patterns from these dimensions. Before making a final fabric choice, be sure that any large patterns or stripes will work well with your pattern shapes.

With right sides facing, hand baste the short ends of the large piece together. Place and pin the zipper along the seam with the tab end 1 inch (2.5 cm) from the raw edge. Stitch the zipper in place with a zipper foot and then reinforce the end with several rows of zigzag

stitches. Remove the hand basting from the zipper section.

Fold the gusset pieces in half widthwise and mark their centers with a pin. Unzip the zipper part of the way. With right sides facing, match the centers and stitch the gussets to each side of the cushion cover. Clip the corners a little for a smoother turn. Turn the pillow right sides out through the zipper opening. Gently ease the corners out and press well. Insert the cushion and zip the zipper closed.

MATERIALS
FOR EACH BACK PILLOW

- pillow
- sturdy fabric
- 1/2 yard (.45 m) contrasting fabric
- used newspaper
- snaps or Velcro (optional)

INSTRUCTIONS

For the pillow back, measure the dimensions of your pillow along the edges. Add 1 inch to the length measurement and then 1/2 inch to each edge for a seam allowance. Cut out a pattern from these dimensions from the newspaper.

For the center pillow front, subtract 5 inches (12 cm) from the length and width measurement and cut out a newspaper pattern to these dimensions. Pin the newspaper pattern onto another sheet of newspaper and measure out a 3-inch (7.5 cm) border for the short sides, then repeat with another 3-inch border for the long sides. Remove the center front pattern, cut out the border strips, and add a 1/2-inch seam allowance to all edges.

Pin the center pillow front and the pillow back patterns to the right side of the fabric and cut out. Repeat with the border patterns, this time using the contrasting fabric. With right sides facing, sew the two short end border strips to the pillow front. Press the seams toward the center of the pillow, then pin and sew the two long border strips. Press again.

With right sides facing, stitch the pillow front and back together, leaving an opening large enough to insert the pillow. Turn right sides out, press well, and insert the pillow. Slipstitch the opening closed. Note: If you anticipate the need for frequent washings, you may want to secure the opening closed with snaps or Velcro.

Playful Insets

Mixing several prints together in one pillow through the use of insets creates smashing designer looks.

MATERIALS
FOR INSET PILLOW

- 2/3 yard (.6 m) of main fabric for inset and pillow back
- 1/4 yard (.2 m) of two additional complementary fabrics
- stuffing

MATERIALS
FOR PAINTED PILLOW

- 2 20-inch squares of fabric
- 1 yard contrasting cording
- disappearing fabric pen
- embroidery floss and/or fabric paint and small craft paintbrush
- foam pillow insert or stuffing

INSTRUCTIONS
FOR BOTH PILLOWS

Cut a 10-inch (25 cm) square and a 14-inch (36 cm) square from the main fabric. Cut four 2- x 14-inch (5 x 36 cm) strips from one of the remaining fabrics, and four 3- x 18-inch (7.5 x 46 cm) strips from the last fabric.

With right sides facing, sew narrow strips to the inset piece and miter the corners. (Refer to page 15 for mitering instructions if needed.) Add the wider strips in the same way. Press all seams.

With right sides facing, stitch all four seams of the two squares together, leaving a small opening for stuffing. Trim the corner seams and turn right sides out. Stuff the pillow tightly, then slip-stitch the opening closed.

Silk Crewel Pillows

The special appeal of these embroidered silk pillows was created by adding light highlights with fabric paint around the crewel work.

MATERIALS

FOR EACH PILLOW

- 2 15-inch (39 cm) squares of silk fabric
- crewel threads in assorted shades of blue, gold, and brown
- fabric paints (optional)
- stuffing

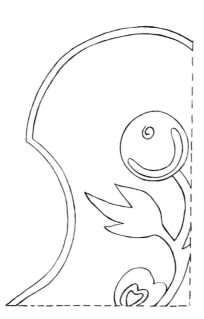

INSTRUCTIONS

Transfer the pattern onto the pillow front. Work the motifs, then add highlights if desired with well-thinned fabric paint. With right sides facing, stitch all four pillow edges, leaving an opening large enough for turning. Trim the seams and turn right sides out. Stuff the pillow gently, then slipstitch the opening closed.

Chair Pillow

Purchased chair pillows can be difficult to find in suitable sizes and colors, not to mention their often-prohibitive costs. In just a few hours, though, you can create custom pillows to add comfort and beauty to any chair in your home.

MATERIALS
- unfolded newspaper
- 1-1/2 yard (1.25 m) fabric
- stuffing

INSTRUCTIONS

Place the unfolded newspaper over the seat of your chair and trace the outline, taking care to mark areas where there are supports or other surface variations. Add a 1/2 inch (12 mm) seam allowance all the way around the outline. Cut out the pattern and then use it to cut out two pieces of fabric.

For the skirt, measure the front and side edges of your chair. Add 1 inch (2.5 cm) for the seam allowance plus 3 inches (7.5 cm) for each pleat you would like. Cut out a strip of fabric that is 6 inches (15 cm) wide and your calculated measurement long.

Make a narrow hem on both short edges and one of the long edges of the skirt. Working from the center outward, pin the skirt with right sides facing to the right side of the cushion back, folding the pleats in even intervals as you work. Hand-baste the skirt in place and turn out to doublecheck the effect.

Cut two tie ends measuring 4 x 7 inches (10 x 18 cm) for each tie end. Fold them in half lengthwise and stitch the long edge and one of the short edges. Turn right sides out and press. With right sides facing, pin the tie ends to the marked areas with the unfinished edge in the seam.

Pin the front and back cushion pieces together with right sides facing. Doublecheck that sections of the skirt and ties haven't slipped out of place, then sew all four seams, leaving a 5-inch (13 cm) opening for turning. Turn right sides out and press well. Tightly stuff the pillow and then slipstitch the opening closed.

APPENDIX

Showcasing beautiful stitchery on the front of a pillow makes a practical alternative to the more expensive route of framing. As you're assembling a pillow, though, be sure to treat your work with the highest respect: if your piece doesn't match the size called for in the instructions, then by all means adjust the pillow shape to fit your work, not vice versa. Pieces that may be inclined to stretch should be lined with a finer-weave fabric.

Also, after all your hard work, be sure to display the pillow in a location where it won't need frequent laundering.

The following descriptions are designed to help you master a specific technique. As you read through them and try to imagine how they work, remember that it's always harder to read about a new technique than it is to actually do it.

Needlework and Embroidery

CROSS-STITCH

The popularity of cross-stitch is surely owed, at least in part, to its remarkable simplicity. Cross stitches are just simple Xs. They can be worked in just about any order, as long as the upper stitch always crosses the lower stitch in the same direction.

When following a chart, each square represents one cross stitch, and the crosses are made over the thread intersections in your chosen fabric.

CHAIN STITCH

This stitch is used to make borders and motif outlines. Working from back to front, make a running stitch.

From under the fabric, bring the needle back through the stitch, near the top, and make another running stitch.

STEM STITCH

The stem stitch is usually used when making outline stitch with lots of curves. Working from back to front, come up at one point, go to wrong side a short space away.

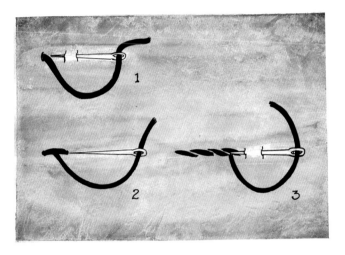

Bring the needle to the front halfway on the first stitch. Insert the needle the same distance as the previous stitch and repeat.

OUTLINE STITCH

The outline stitch is used to surround embroidered areas or to make lines as part of a motif. It is also called a back stitch when one stitch follows another. It is the easiest stitch to make.

Working from back to front, come up at one point, and go down to the wrong side in small, even stitches.

SATIN STITCH

The satin stitch is used to fill in areas with solid stitches. Sometimes it's easier to work from the widest section first and save the narrowest for last.

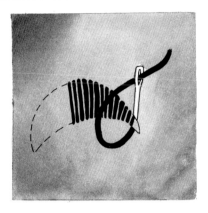

Working from back to front, come up at one point, go down to the wrong side at the designated point. Come up again as close as possible to the original insertion point. Continue until the entire area is filled in.

FRENCH KNOT

French knots are used as the centers of flowers, as buds, or wherever a raised spot of color is required.

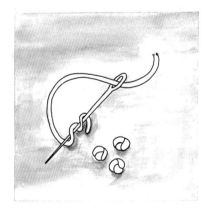

Working from back to front, come up at one point, wrap yarn around the needle from one to three times, depending on how high you want the knot to stand up, and reinsert the needle at the same point.

BULLION STITCH

The bullion stitch is like a long French knot. Working from back to front, insert the needle at the beginning of the line to be covered and reinsert it at the end of the line, leaving a loop.

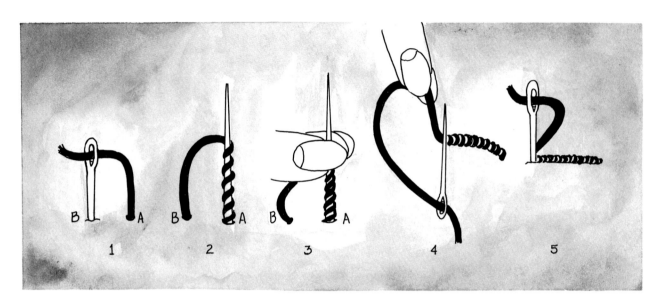

Reinsert the needle at the beginning point and twist around the loop of yarn, pull the needle through the twists and insert the needle at the point where the twisted yarn will lie flat against the fabric.

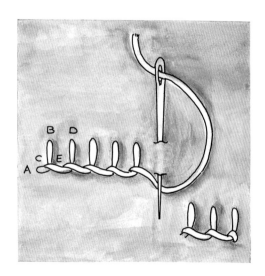

BLANKET STITCH

The blanket stitch makes a lovely edging stitch. It can be worked in the thinnest silk threads for a small, delicate item, or in a thick crewel yarn for larger items. Bring the needle to the right side at Point A and insert it above and to the right at Point B. Bring the needle to the right side again at Point C, with the thread under the needle tip, and pull the thread through. As you repeat the stitches, the last point of the previous stitch will act as the first point of the next stitch.

Quilting

PATCHWORK

Although patchwork can look difficult to a novice, most patterns can be easily pieced by a beginner. Before you begin, study the finished piece to see how it breaks down in shapes (two triangles pieced together to form a square, for instance, or squares set on the diagonal to form diamonds).

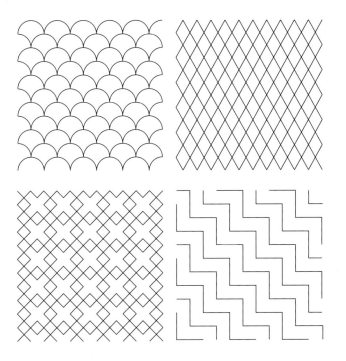

Patchwork can be done quickly with a rotary cutter and assembly line stitching. A rotary cutter allows you to cut through multiple layers of cloth (instead of the traditional two). To assembly line sew, first pin 20 or 30 pieces together and position them in a stack on your sewing machine. Stitch the seams as your normally would, but don't cut the threads in between seams. You will end up with a kitelike streamer of patchwork pieces, which you can clip apart in a minute or two.

With clothing, it often doesn't matter if you sew one seam 5/8 inch and another 1/2 inch — the garment may well still fit fine. With patchwork, though, identical seam allowances are a must for the points to meet. Pressing all seams flat is especially important with patchwork quilting because unpressed or poorly pressed seams will cause unsightly bulk in the finished piece, or, worse, cause the blocks to pull or twist.

APPLIQUÉ

Appliqué is usually used in quilting when you have a shape or motif that would be very difficult to do with geometric patchwork piecing. In this book, you will be provided with an applique pattern. Just cut it out, press under a seam allowance, (clipping the corners if needed for turning ease), and hand baste the shape to a backing fabric. Topstitch or zigzag the motif around the edges and quilt over it as you would patchwork.

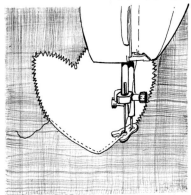

QUILTING

The actual process of quilting, or adding texture though a series of simple running stitches, is not complicated at all — just time intensive. You can shadow quilt your design by outlining the patchwork or appliqued shapes with running stitches — or do an allover pattern. For most of the small quilting projects in this book, you won't need a hoop or large frame to keep the fabric taut. An increasingly popular option to hand quilting is machine quilting.

Hand Work

DRAWN THREAD WORK

A combination of strategic thread removal and embroidery, drawn thread work is easier to work than it sounds. The first step is to mark the area where you plan to remove the threads. You can do this with a disappearing fabric marker (pretest on a swatch first, especially if you've chosen an expensive fabric) or by outlining the area with loose running stitches.

The next step is to make a few cuts in the center of your marked area so you can begin removing threads. The tip of a tapestry needle can be quite helpful with this step. After the threads are removed from the marked area, their ends will need to be secured with a buttonhole stitch to prevent unwanted unraveling. Tack the loose threads on the wrong side of the buttonhole stitch (if working with a small area) or create an inch or two or running threads on the back side of the fabric (if working with a larger area). From this point you begin embroidering, following a chosen chart or graph for specific stitches and patterns.

FILET CROCHET

Filet crochet is characterized by a series of open and filled squares, with the filled squares creating a motif in the finished piece. Most filet crochet is worked in squares formed by parallel sides on one double crochet with a top and bottom made from 2 chain stitches. For this most common type of filet crochet, begin with a chain base. The chain base will need 3 chain stitches for each square of the motif plus 1 extra chain for the double crochet at the end. When following a chart, remember that the last stitch of one square is the first stitch of the next. The first row after the foundation chain begins with a chain 3 for the outside edge of the first square.

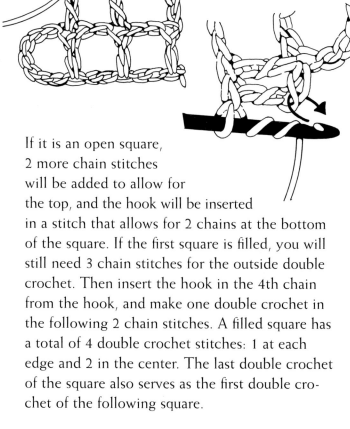

If it is an open square, 2 more chain stitches will be added to allow for the top, and the hook will be inserted in a stitch that allows for 2 chains at the bottom of the square. If the first square is filled, you will still need 3 chain stitches for the outside double crochet. Then insert the hook in the 4th chain from the hook, and make one double crochet in the following 2 chain stitches. A filled square has a total of 4 double crochet stitches: 1 at each edge and 2 in the center. The last double crochet of the square also serves as the first double crochet of the following square.

CUTWORK

Begin by transferring your chosen motif to the
fabric. Place the fabric in an embroidery hoop.
Make two rows of short running stitches on the
right side of the fabric along the pattern design.
The first row should be about 1/16 inch inside the
edge, and the second row should run closer to the
edge of the design line, about 1/32 of an inch.
The running stitches reinforce the fabric and provide a guideline for the buttonhole stitches.

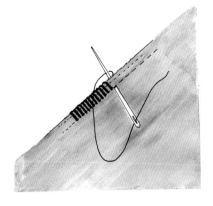

Next, secure a length of thread on the back
side of the fabric at the beginning of the row.
Insert the needle from back to front beneath the
outer row. Point the needle toward the design
line and cross the thread under the needle at the
edge of the line. Pull the needle through and
repeat across the row. For corners, work the
stitches to the edge the same length, while fan-
ning the lower part of the stitch out around the
corner. For a point, make the inside stitches
closer together. All stitches should face the space
that will be cut away.

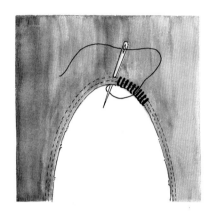

When the main design areas have been
worked, cut the spaces away with sharp-pointed
applique or embroidery scissors by carefully
inserting the scissors from the back of the work.
Cut several slits to the sides and corners to create
a series of flaps. Roll the flaps back to the stitches
and then carefully trim them away.

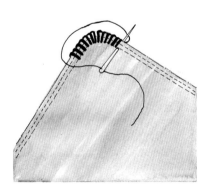

index

ADDITIONAL CONTRIBUTORS

Suzanne Koppi, Nola Theiss, Joyce Cusick, Juanita Metcalf, Diane Grinnell, Evan Bracken, and Pamela Whitlock.